How to Understand Judaism

Marcus Braybrooke

How to Understand Judaism

SCM PRESS LTD

Copyright © Marcus Braybrooke 1995

Map by John Flower

0 334 02614 8

First published in 1995
by SCM Press Ltd,
9–17 St Albans Place N1 0NX

Typeset at The Spartan Press Ltd,
Lymington, Hants
and printed in Great Britain by
Redwood Books, Trowbridge, Wilts

To
The International Council
of
Christians and Jews
and
The Council
of
Christians and Jews

Contents

Preface   xiii

1   What is Judaism?   1

What do you do when you study a religion?   1

Jews in a changing world   3
  Mobility   1
  Out of the ghetto   4
  Jewish identity   5

2   Passover and Shavuot   7

Passover   7
  The special foods   7
  What happens?   8
  What is remembered?   9

Chosen people   10

Shavuot   11

3   The Jewish Year   13

The High Holy Days   13
  Rosh Hashanah   13
  Yom Kippur   16
  Sukkot   17

Minor festivals   17
  Chanukah   17
  Purim   19

Fast days   21

Other special days   21

Holocaust Day: Yom Ha'Shoah   21
Israel Independence Day: Yom Ha'atzmaut   21
The New Year of Trees: Tu B'Shevat   22

4   The Home and the Sabbath   23

The home   23

Mezuzah   23
Special clothes   24

Kosher   25

The Sabbath   26

Jewish feelings about the Sabbath   26
What happens on the Sabbath?   26
What work is forbidden on the Sabbath?   27
The meaning of Sabbath observance   27

5   Rites of Passage   29

Circumcision   29

Barmitzvah and Batmitzvah   31

Marriage   32

Jewish teaching about marriage   32
The wedding   33

Burial   35

Mourning   35
Resurrection   36

6   The Synagogue   37

Inside a synagogue   37

The origins of the synagogue   38
Schul   39

Synagogue worship   40
   The morning service   40

The rabbi   40

Prayer and study   40
   Prayer   40
   Mystical Judaism   41
   Study   42

7   Torah and Jewish Literature   43

What does Torah mean?   43

Revelation   44

Respect for scripture   46

How is Torah interpreted in daily life?   46

The rabbinic literature   48

Later writings   49
   Translations, texts and commentaries   49
   Responsa   50
   Prayer books   50
   Zohar   51

Other literature   51

8   From 1800 BCE to 1800 CE   52

Beginnings   52
   Abraham   53
   Moses   54

The development of rabbinic Judaism   57
   Ezra   57
   The Pharisees and the rabbis   58
   Babylon   58

Under Islam   59

The later Middle Ages   59
   Poland   59

9　**Jews in the Modern World**　　61

　The rights of man　　61

　The nineteenth century　　62

　　France　　62
　　Britain　　62
　　Germany　　63
　　Poland　　63
　　Hungary　　64

　The twentieth century: the spread of antisemitism　　64

　After the Holocaust　　64

　　Poland　　66
　　Romania　　66
　　Hungary　　66
　　Russia　　66
　　France　　68
　　Britain　　68

　New centres of Jewish life　　69

　　USA　　69
　　Israel　　70

　The future　　71

10　**Varieties of Judaism**　　72

　Orthodox or Traditional Judaism　　72

　Progressive Judaism　　74

　　Reform Judaism　　74
　　Conservative Judaism　　75
　　Reconstructionist Judaism　　75
　　Humanistic Judaism　　75
　　Liberal Judaism　　76

　Unity and difference within Judaism　　76

　　The Messiah　　76
　　Zionism　　77
　　Internal differences　　77

11 A New Relationship 78

Antisemitism 78

Anti-Zionism 78

Anti-Judaism 79

A new relationship 81
Jesus the Jew 81
Covenant 82

Conclusion 83

Bibliography 84

Glossary 86

Index 91

Preface

It is a risky undertaking to write about a religion other than one's own. Beyond the proper desire for accuracy and fairness, there is the more difficult task of beginning to feel what it might be like to belong to that religion. Yet, if we do not attempt to do this, we remain outsiders to that which offers the deepest inspiration to our neighbours' lives. I hope this book will encourage many Christians and others to a greater appreciation of Judaism and to a desire to get to know their Jewish neighbours better.

I am very grateful to many Jews and Christians, especially members of the International Council of Christians and Jews and the Council of Christians and Jews, who have helped me to understand more about both Judaism and my own faith.

I am particularly grateful to Rabbi Dr Jonathan Romain for reading the text and for his comments. I am also grateful to Westminster College, Oxford, for allowing me to use some material prepared for one of their distance learning courses, and to friends who have looked out photographs for me. I am again grateful to Revd Dr John Bowden and to Margaret Lydamore and Stephen Rogers also of SCM Press for their help and to my wife Mary for her support.

To avoid an undue amount of italics only unusual transliterated Hebrew words are printed in italics. More familiar words – and the decision on which words fall into this category is bound to be arbitrary – are in ordinary print. There is a glossary and I am grateful to Rabbi Dr Jonathan Romain for allowing me to base this on the glossary which appears in his *Faith and Practice: A Guide to Reform Judaism Today*, published by the Reform Synagogues of Great Britain 1991.

Marcus Braybrooke

May 1995

Acknowledgments

Photographs are reproduced courtesy:

Bristol and West Progressive Congregation (1, 22); Hulton Deutsch (2, 28, 29, 30, 32); Robert Harding Picture Library (5); Laurence Salzman (8, 15); Jewish Museum of Budapest (10, 24); Keith Glasgow (11); Juliette Soester (12); Sonia Halliday Photographs (13); Helen Tann (14); Nick Evans (16); Meir and Nava Agam (17); Rabbi Jonathan Romain (18, 23); Polish Embassy (19); Metropolitan Museum of Art (27); Mary Evans Picture Library (31); Andes Press (33); West London Synagogue (34); London Auschwitz Exhibition Group 1982 (35); Imperial War Museum (36); Louis Reems (37); Arturo Mari (38); Rabbi Hadassah Davis (16); Tony Reese (1, 22); Sir Sigmund Sternberg (38); Barry Searle (13).

1

What is Judaism?

Lord, what does my being Jewish mean to You?

What do you do when you study a religion?

The study of a religion has many facets. It will include study of sacred scriptures, discussion of a religion's ethical teaching, awareness of rituals, an introduction to its history and much more.

Because some scholars emphasize one element and some another, there are different ways of describing a religion. In this book we try to capture a sense of the many ways of being Jewish in the contemporary world.

Generalization is dangerous. What is true for some Jews in one part of the world today may not be true for others. In any case, as it is often said in jest, 'where you have two Jews, you have three opinions'.

We shall begin by learning about festivals, about ceremonies at birth, marriage and death, and about the life of the home and the synagogue. It is by participation in such occasions that a Jewish child learns what it means to be Jewish. Most people do not learn their own religion primarily from a formal course of instruction, even if they do attend one, but from sharing in festivals, worship and rites of passage. From these one can pick up a knowledge

of central beliefs in Judaism and of decisive events in Jewish history, but it will be necessary to look again at Jewish history and teaching in a more systematic way.

Often it is easier to acquire 'external' knowledge than to begin to appreciate what the religion means to its adherents. For this you need 'empathy' or a willingness to try to understand the other from that person's point of view, rather than judging from one's own standpoint. This means that it is helpful to meet with and talk with some Jews about their religion. In many places there are organized meetings for discussion between Jews and Christians. A visit to a synagogue will be valuable. Novels also give you a feel for Jewish life. Jewish newspapers, such as *Forward*, which is published in the USA, or the *Jewish Chronicle*, which is published in Britain, are interesting to read.

In studying another religion we need to try to avoid seeing it through our own spectacles. For that reason, comparisons have been avoided, especially because for centuries Christians have used Judaism as the backdrop to their own story of salvation. The final chapter describes the new relationship between Jews and Christians that has been developed since the Holocaust.

1. At his Barmitzvah, a boy affirms his Jewish identity

Lord, what does my being Jewish mean to You? What lessons are You teaching me in the triumphs and tragedies of our history? Why do we wander from land to land, to find our rest in You?

Help me to recognize Your presence in Jewish prayer, and Your love in our laughter. Bring Your forgiveness to our failings, and Your constancy to our suffering.

And when I or those I love lose heart or get discouraged, renew Your work of redemption in us. Plant again in us the honesty of our prophets, and the faithfulness of our teachers and martyrs. Renew the compassion and kindness of Your people.

Lord help us not to use these gifts for vanity or self-glory, but to bring joy into the world, and a Jewish blessing to all Your children.

From the British Reform Jewish Prayer Book, Vol III,
Forms of Prayer for Jewish Worship, Days of Awe,
The Reform Synagogues of Great Britain 1985, p. 411

David's mother asked 'Did your highty-tighty *goyim* (gentile) friends give you a nice tea?'

'I had strawberries and cream', he said rapturously.

'And bacon sandwiches?'

'Don't be daft, Mother.'

'Who is being daft? After you've taken one step, it's easy to take another. You want proof? Have a look in the mirror?'

For a moment David did not understand. Then he knew she was reminding him of how he had cut off his sidelocks before starting at high school. A new chapter had been opening for him and he did not intend to begin it with a handicap.

Maisie Mosco, *Almonds and Raisins*, Hodder Coronet Edition 1993, p. 106

Jews in a changing world

For many centuries between the destruction of the second Temple in 70 CE (Common Era)* until the beginnings of Jewish emancipation in the nineteenth century, a sense of timelessness prevailed. Jews were driven from one country to another, but they remained a united people, set apart from other nations. Virtually all Jews accepted the authority of the Torah, which combined the biblical written law and the oral teaching of the rabbis of the early centuries of the Common Era. Jews used to live in enclosed, largely self-governing communities.

From the eighteenth century, the Jewish world has undergone profound changes. The percentage of Jews living in Europe has declined very sharply. Today, most Jews live in the wider community and quite a number no longer practise or observe their religion.

* The abbreviation CE (Common Era) and BCE (Before the Common Era) are more appropriate than BC (Before Christ) and AD (Anno Domini – in the Year of the Lord).

2. Jewish shoemakers in the Warsaw Ghetto.

Mobility

'The wandering Jew' is a proverbial term. From the time of the exile in Babylon in the sixth century BCE, the majority of Jews have lived outside Israel in what is known as the Diaspora. Jews have often moved from country to country. Sometimes this was for trade. Often Jews had to flee persecution and political changes. For nearly two thousand years, until this century, they have had no country of their own.

There are differences, therefore, amongst Jews because of the country from which their family originates. One distinction is between those descended from the Jews of Spain (from where they were expelled in 1492) who are known as Sephardi, and those, known as Ashkenazi, whose ancestors lived in Eastern Europe.

In the last one hundred years there have been great migrations of Jews, especially from Europe to America and Israel. In 1860, nearly 90% of the world's Jews lived in Europe. Today only 20% do so. In 1939 there were about nine and a half million Jews living in Europe. By 1990, the figure was only a little over two million. Europe's leadership of the Jewish world has now passed to Israel and the USA.

The main reason for this change is persecution. Many Jews in Eastern Europe in the nineteenth and early twentieth century were either killed in pogroms or forced to seek a new life in Western Europe or the USA. At that time America's doors were open to European immigrants. The largest Jewish community is now in the USA. Antisemitism also encouraged the growth of Zionism and the desire for a Jewish state.

In this century the worst persecution of all took place under the Nazis who controlled most of continental Europe. Some six million Jews were killed in what is known as the Holocaust or the Shoah. Many others fled for their lives.

Some survivors made their way to Israel. Other Jews have come to Israel from many parts of the world, including large numbers from Arab countries. Israel has now become home for over four million Jews. Some have come to seek security after the terrible sufferings of the Holocaust in Europe. Antisemitism is a recurrent danger of which Jews are always aware. Others had to flee persecution in some Muslim countries. Many emigrated to Israel, or made *aliyah*, from a wish to live a fully Jewish life in a country which is Jewish.

Out of the ghetto

In the Middle Ages, most Jews lived in Jewish quarters, often called ghettos. From early in the last century restrictions began to be lifted ('emancipation'). Jews in Western Europe were allowed to enter fully into national life. For example in Britain, by the second half of the nineteenth century, Jews had won the right to sit as members of Parliament and some Jews were received at court.

To gain acceptance into the wider society, some Jews adapted their way of life to fit in with that society. Each Jew had to make his or her own decision about how to practise his or her Jewishness, which is another reason for increasing variety. Some Jews found that they could not always observe all the requirements of the Torah (Law).

Now as many Jews mix freely in the wider society, the question of 'marrying out' has become increasingly significant. In the USA in 1920, the intermarriage rate was estimated at only 1%. A survey published in 1991, suggested that more than 50% of young married American Jews had chosen a non-Jewish spouse. If the woman is a non-Jew, the children will not count as Jews. This has caused worries about the continuity of the Jewish community. One American writer has even suggested that a Jew today is someone with Jewish grandchildren!

It was not just a matter of individual compromise or adaptation. As different movements within Judaism appeared, so different ways of interpreting Torah emerged. The unity of the mediaeval Jewish world has been broken with the development of Progressive Judaism. The situation now is more akin to the pluralism of the Jewish world of the first century CE.

Today, there are various expressions of Orthodox Judaism: Hasidic, Traditional, Neo-Orthodox. Amongst the Progressive or non-Orthodox, there are Conservative, Reconstructionist, Reform, Liberal and even Humanistic Jews. In chapter 10, we shall look at the differences in more detail.

All this should make clear that there are many ways of being Jewish. The story is told of a rabbi who was asked to speak to a Christian audience. She arrived a little early and as no one took much notice of her, she sat quietly at the back. After a while the chairman apologized that they were not ready to start, but they were still waiting for the rabbi. They had expected a man with a large hat and a flowing beard, not a fashionably dressed young woman!

Jewish identity

Visitors to Israel are sometimes surprised that in the Jewish state only a minority are religiously observant, even if religious Jews have considerable influence on the society. There are many Jews who value their history and culture, but who are not religious. It has been said that in the USA the modern synagogue may be more of a community centre than a building consecrated solely for divine worship and study. Increasingly Jews, especially in America, see themselves as an ethnic group rather than a religious community.

Whilst most Jews have a deep attachment to and concern for Israel, Jews of Europe and America usually participate fully in the society where they live. This means that the Jewish community in France or Hungary or the Netherlands or Denmark, for example, each has its own distinctive character.

3. Jews at the Western Wall in Jerusalem

What a constantly enigmatic, unique phenomenon in the history of religions and of the world this Judaism is – for others as well as for itself. Its nature is almost impossible to define . . .

– A state and yet not a state! Why not? Because since the Babylonian exile (586 BCE) a majority . . . of Jews have lived outside the 'Holy Land'.

– A people and yet not a people! Why not? Because unlike any other people this people is an international entity. Countless Jews feel that politically and culturally they are Americans, English, French, or German and by no means 'Israelis abroad'.

– A race and yet not a race! Why not? Because already from late Roman times individuals from every possible tribe and people have become Jews by marriage or conversion; some Eastern Jews are descended from the Turkish people of the Chasars and yet others from the black Falashas in Ethiopia, so that present-day Israel has become a manifestly multi-racial state with men and women of every possible colour of skin, hair and eyes.

– A linguistic community and yet not a linguistic community! Why not? Because Judaism knows neither a culture nor a language common to all Jews. Many Jews know neither Hebrew nor Yiddish.

– A religious community and yet not a religious community! Why not? Because a large number of Jews – even in Israel – do not believe in God and claim their Jewishness has nothing to do with religion; others are indeed religious but personally reject observance of the halakhah [or Jewish law].

Hans Kung, *Judaism*, SCM Press and Crossroad 1992, pp. 19–20

2

Passover and Shavuot

Why is this night different from all other nights?

Passover

For many Jewish children one of their first memories will be of sharing in, and perhaps partly sleeping through, the Passover or Pesach meal.

The special foods

There is much preparation for this special evening. Before Passover all leaven or *chametz* has to be destroyed. 'For seven days no leaven bread shall be found in your house (Ex. 12.15).' The house is thoroughly cleaned. Special cooking utensils and china are used for Passover. The night before Passover, the parents hide a few pieces of bread in different parts of the house and the children have to look for them. Then the next day the leavened bread is burnt.

There is a traditional order for the evening's ritual, which is called the seder, a term which is sometimes used of the whole event. Before the Passover meal, the table is carefully prepared. Each item of food is a symbol recalling part of the story of how God delivered the children of Israel from slavery in Egypt.

Matzo (plural matzot) is unleavened bread, which takes very little time to bake. This is the bread the children of Israel made when they were in a hurry to leave Egypt. It is also the 'bread of affliction' which they ate whilst they were slaves in Egypt.

The matzot have an important place in the seder.

Three matzot are arranged between the folds of a white cloth so that they do not touch each other. At the beginning of the passover seder, the middle matzo is broken by the head of the house. Half of this, called the afikomen, is hidden until after the supper.

The bread is raised while the father says, 'This is the bread of affliction which our ancestors ate in the land of Egypt. Let all who are hungry come and eat. Let all who are in need come and celebrate Passover. This year, we are here: next year in the land of Israel. This year we are slaves: next year, free men.'

During the seder, everyone drinks four cups of *wine*. These are reminders of the four ways that God spoke about setting the Israelites free:

I will bring you out,

I will deliver you

I will redeem you,

I will take you to me (Ex. 6.6–7).

At the beginning of the evening the first cup of wine is filled and, after a blessing, drunk, whilst participants recline on their left side, as a sign that they are free men and women. In the ancient world free people would recline to eat. A symbol of this is the cushion that is placed next to the person conducting the seder. This is another reminder that this is a festival of freedom.

Three other cups of wine are drunk.

As each of the ten plagues are recalled, participants dip a finger in the cup and spill a drop of

4. An eighteenth century Seder table,
   preserved in Budapest

wine, recalling the sufferings of the Egyptians.

On the seder dish there will be:

Salt water or vinegar, in which some of the food is dipped. Salt calls to mind the tears of the slaves. It also is a reminder of the Red (or Reed) Sea which the Israelites crossed on dry land, but in which their Egyptian pursuers were drowned;

Charoset, which is a mixture of crushed almonds and apples, sprinkled with cinnamon and wine. It looks like mud and represents the mud bricks which the Israelite slaves had to make. Almonds and apples were some of the fruits of the Promised Land, so charoset may also symbolize the Promised Land;

Bitter Herbs. Various vegetables are used for these, such as horseradish, but long lettuce leaves are ideal. The leaves are crisp and pleasant, but they grow from a stalk which is bitter. The bitter stalk represents slavery and the crisp leaves stand for freedom;

Carpas. A sweet herb or vegetable to be dipped in salt water. The word is made up of the letters of the Hebrew word for hard labour – another reminder of slavery. Carpas is dipped in salt water to commemorate the bunch of hyssop which the Israelites dipped in the blood of the Pesach sacrifice to smear on their doorposts. The greenery also represents the spring season at which Passover occurs.

There is also a burnt *bone* on the seder plate. This is a reminder of the Paschal offering, which used to be made whilst the Temple still stood. It is not eaten.

The roast *egg* represents the sacrificial offerings that the Israelites used to present in the Temple.

There is also an actual meal, but not usually lamb.

There are slight variations and different meanings are sometimes given to the symbols.

What happens?

Why is this night different?

The pattern of the evening's observance or seder is set down in a book, of which there are many different versions, some in Hebrew, some in English, some for adults, some for children.

Early in the Passover seder usually the youngest child present asks the great question:

'Why is this night different from all other nights?'

'On all other nights, we can eat bread or matzo: why tonight only matzo?'

'On all other nights we can eat any kind of herbs: why, tonight, bitter herbs?'

'On all other nights, we don't dip the herbs we eat into anything: why tonight, do we dip them twice?'

'On all other nights, we can eat either sitting up, straight or reclining: why tonight do we all recline?'

Usually the child will have learned these questions beforehand and may sing them to an ancient melody.

The traditional answer to the child's question, given by the leader of the seder, goes something like this:

'Our ancestors were slaves to Pharoah in Egypt, but God brought us out from there, "with a strong hand and an outstretched arm". If the Holy One, Blessed be He, had not brought our ancestors out of Egypt, we, and our children, and our children's children would still be slaves to Pharaoh in Egypt. So even if we were all wise and clever and old and learned in the Torah, it would still be our duty to tell the story of the Exodus from Egypt. The more one talks about the Exodus, the more praiseworthy it is.'

Although the seder recalls events long ago, each participant is meant to feel that he or she experienced God's deliverance. 'In every generation every Jew must feel as if he himself came out of Egypt.'

The seder speaks of four sons: the wise son, the wicked son, the simple son and the son who has no capacity to enquire. The wicked sons asks, 'What do you mean by this service?' The seder commentary says of him, 'By the expression *you*, it is clear he does not include himself since he has excluded himself from the collective body of the nation.' He is told that 'This is done because of what the Lord did for *me* when I went forth from Egypt: for *me* but not for *him*; for had he been there he would not have been thought worthy to be redeemed.' To the simple son, the whole story is told, saying 'because of what the Lord did for me, when I went forth from Egypt'.

What is remembered?

The story of how God rescued the Israelites from slavery in Egypt is told in the book of Exodus. Critical historians have questioned much of the biblical narrative. The Passover seder includes some further traditional material.

5. Yemenite Jews observe Passover

The book of Exodus tells of the birth of Moses, his miraculous survival, his upbringing at the Egyptian court, his concern for justice, his flight to Midian, the revelation of God, the return to Egypt, the challenge to Pharaoh, the ten plagues, the Passover, the Exodus, the Crossing of the Sea. But notice the Passover seder scarcely mentions Moses. It is God who rescues the children of Israel.

A song, called the *Dayenu*, which is sung after the meal, sums up what is remembered and the many reasons that the Jews have to be thankful to God.

You may have some sympathy for the Egyptians. There is a midrash (story) recounting how when the Israelites started singing and rejoicing at their rescue from the Red Sea God asked, 'How can you sing whilst my children are drowning in the Sea?' The Egyptians are also God's children.

Jews take part in a Passover seder with varying motives:

1. It brings the family together.
2. It reaffirms Jewish identity as 'chosen people'.
3. It is a festival of freedom. Jews have known persecution in every century. Often at Passover, Jews who are still the victims of oppression are remembered. In the 1970s and 1980s special thought was given to the Jews of Russia and sometimes Jews in the West tried to telephone them.
4. It recalls God's past mercies.
5. It encourages participants to experience God's mercy to them.
6. Through centuries of exile it has reaffirmed Jewish links with the land of Israel. The ceremony ends with the words 'next year in Jerusalem'.
7. It points forward to liberation for all people. After the end of the meal the door is flung open wide for the prophet Elijah, who will come one day as a messenger of the messianic future. There is a Jewish mystical saying that 'We should also pray for the wicked among the peoples of the world; we should love them too. As long as we do not pray in this way, as long as we do not love in this way, the Messiah will not come.'

Chosen people

The claim to be 'a chosen people' has been a cause of prejudice and antisemitism. It not only puzzles or even shocks some Gentiles but is at times an embarrassment to some modern Jews. Indeed the Reconstructionists, a Reform Movement founded by Rabbi Mordecai Kaplan in the USA, have even removed the words 'chosen people' from their prayer books.

It is stressed that the choice of Israel is an expression of God's everlasting love. In Hosea 11.1 God says 'When Israel was a child, I loved him and out of Egypt I called my son.' Some passages in the Torah suggest that the Covenant is conditional upon obedience. Exodus 22.31 says, 'You are to be my holy people.' The Rabbis commented, 'If you are holy, only then are you Mine.'

It is clear that at times the sense of being chosen has been used in an exclusive way and has been an occasion for pride. Many ancient texts speak of non-Jews as *ha-goyim*, in the way that Greeks spoke of others as barbarians and that European imperialists looked down on and exploited other races. Jews in the ancient world regarded others as polytheistic and idolatrous and one way of maintaining a distinct identity is to keep oneself apart, in the way

6. Seder dishes from Eastern Europe

that non-smokers may not allow smoking in their homes or some vegetarians will not eat with meat eaters.

The hope that others would come to worship the one God was usually an eschatological one, that is to say something that would happen at the end of the age. By Hellenistic and Roman times, however, there was a considerable missionary effort and a large number of Gentiles, even if they did not convert and become proselytes, were 'God-fearers', who accepted the monotheism and high moral teaching of Judaism.

It is in modern times that there has been some unease with the concept of being *the* chosen people. As Judaism today encounters other world faiths in a more open dialogue, there is an emphasis on the universalist elements of Jewish teaching. The fact that God made one man Adam, from whom all humans are descended, is seen to teach the basic unity of the human family and means that no one may say to another person, 'My ancestor was greater than your ancestor.' It is pointed out that before God made a covenant with Abraham, he first made a covenant with Noah. The rabbis spoke of the seven commandments given to Noah, which were incumbent upon all people. These seven commandments are Laws, which implied the establishment of courts and a system of justice, and the prohibition of idolatry, blasphemy, sexual immorality, bloodshed, theft and the taking of a limb from a living animal.

Blessed art thou, Lord our God and King of the Universe, who hast chosen us among all peoples and hast set us apart among all tongues and hast sanctified us with thy commandments, and who in thy love hast given feasts for our joy – this feast day of unleavened bread, the day of our freedom and happiness, devoted to a holy assembly and the remembrance of the departure from Egypt. Thou art the one who hast chosen us and sanctified us beyond other nations and given us joy and gladness for an inheritance. Blessed art thou, Lord, who sanctifies Israel and the feasts.

Traditional Passover prayer

In general, most Jews today would say that Judaism does not claim an exclusive way to God (and they criticize Christians for such a claim). They would say that it is the religion into which they have been born and that it is the best one for them. Generally, Jews now would understand their mission as one of example, 'to be a light to lighten the Gentiles'. Nonetheless, conversion to Judaism is possible – rather more easily to Progressive Judaism – and a number of conversions take place each year.

Shavuot

The Feast of Weeks, which is called Shavuot, is a harvest festival, but also commemorates the giving of the Torah on Mount Sinai seven weeks after the departure from Egypt. In the Bible, Shavuot is purely an agricultural festival, marking the end of the barley harvest and the start of the wheat harvest.

The biblical references are Ex. 23.14–17; 34.22; Lev. 23.9–22 and Deut. 16.9–12.

The name 'Weeks' refers to the timing of the festival, which is held exactly seven weeks after Passover. It is sometimes referred to by its Greek name, Pentecost, which signifies that it is the feast of the fiftieth day (Lev. 23.15–21).

After the destruction of the Temple, the ceremonial counting of days continued and the whole period became known as *sefirah*, counting or *omer* season. It came to be a time of austerity when it was considered improper to celebrate marriages, to cut one's hair or to wear new clothes.

One explanation for this austerity is the story that thousands of disciples of the famous second-century Rabbi Akiva died of a plague during this period. The period recalls other tragedies in Jewish history, such as the Rhineland massacres during the Crusades. It is also the period in which the Holocaust Memorial Day is set.

Three days are allowed to interrupt the sombre mood.

One is the anniversary of the establishment of the state of Israel.

The second is *Lag ba-Omer* when the restrictions are suspended and the children light bonfires and shoot arrows. This may be because it commemorates the day on which the plague among Rabbi Akiva's students ended, or because it was the day on which Bar Kochba, a Jewish freedom fighter active around 130 CE, won a victory against the Romans. It is also traditionally regarded as the day on which Rabbi Simeon ben Yochai, the founder of Jewish mysticism, died (*c.* 150 CE).

The third is *Yom Yerushalayim*, which commemorates the reunification of the city during the Six Day War in 1967.

The Torah calls Shavuot 'the day of the first fruit', *Yom Habikkurim*, because farmers would bring the first of their harvest to Jerusalem as a token of thanksgiving to God. As long as the Temple stood, every pilgrim was required to bring a sheaf (omer) to give to the priest in the Temple as well as the first fruits of other crops (*bikkurim*). Although the offering of first fruits is no longer observed – for many centuries Jews did not have their own land – fruits and vegetables are still associated with the festival.

The festival also recalls the giving of the ten commandments. According to Exodus 19.1, the children of Israel, after escaping from Egypt, came to the wilderness of Sinai 'in the third month'. The people consecrated themselves, whilst Moses went up to the top of Mount Sinai and was given the ten commandments (see Ex. 19). The celebration of the festival includes both the reading of the Decalogue and also the book of Ruth.

In the Middle Ages it became customary to introduce children to the study of the Law on Shavuot. At dawn the father would bring his child to the synagogue. The child sat before his teacher. Between them lay a tablet with all the letters of the Hebrew alphabet. The teacher would read each letter, which the child would repeat after him. A spot of honey sat on every letter and the child licked the honey from each letter as he learned it. The young student was then presented with a honey cake with a Torah verse on it. At the conclusion of the lesson the child read the verse and ate the cake. It is customary at Shavuot to eat dairy products, especially cheese cake.

Hebrew

The Hebrew alphabet has 22 letters and no vowels. Five letters are written differently if they come at the end of a word (inside box). Hebrew is written from right to left. If this were a Hebrew book it would start at the back. Hebrew is the language in which the Old Testament was first written. It is the language of Israel today.

7. The Hebrew alphabet

3

The Jewish Year

Our religion has three elements: awe, love and joy, by each of which we can draw near to God.

Judah Halevi

Jewish self-understanding has been shaped by a rich, if chequered, history. The festivals that are observed each year keep this history alive.

The Jewish calendar is a lunar one, so that from time to time an extra month is added to keep the Jewish year in step with the solar year. The system was permanently established under Hillel II, who was the Patriarch of Palestinian Jewry in about 360 CE.

Two traditions can be recognized in the Bible about when the year begins. One is a nomadic-pastoral one, which says of the spring month, 'This month shall be for you the beginning of months' (Ex. 12.2). The other is a settled-agricultural one, which refers to the autumn harvest as 'the end of the year' (Ex. 23.16). This tradition in time became the stronger, so that the autumn festival came to mark the new year.

The High Holy Days

Rosh Hashanah

The New Year festival is called Rosh Hashanah. Although it is customary to eat apples and honey as a sign of the hope that the coming year will be 'good and sweet', the New Year is a time of judgment,

preceded by a period of repentance. On Rosh Hashanah, people individually and the nations collectively are judged by God, who is omniscient and omnipotent. It is, therefore, more appropriate to wish friends 'a good New Year', rather than 'a happy New Year'.

The origins of Rosh Hashanah go back to the book of Exodus. Moses had joyously ascended Mount Sinai to receive the Law, but by the time he came back down from the mountain, forty days later, the Jews had started worshipping a golden calf. In his anger, Moses broke the tablets of the Law. Moses then climbed the mountain again to ask God to pardon the Jewish people. After his return, God told him once more to climb the mountain. Forty days later, on the tenth day of the month of Tishri, Moses returned with the second tablets – a tangible sign of God's forgiveness and love. This is now the Day of Atonement, Yom Kippur.

The first day of the month of Tishri is the start of the New Year, Rosh Hashanah. It is marked by the blowing of the shofar, a ram's horn. Just as a trumpet proclaims a king, so the shofar heralds the King of Kings. The ram's horn also is a reminder of Abraham's willingness to sacrifice his son Isaac (Gen. 22.13 says that God provided a ram for the sacrifice).

Special foods are eaten at many festivals. Each

family will have its own traditions and many families no longer have time to keep up all the old customs. There are also various explanations for some of the traditions. The New Year itself is a good example of some special festival foods.

During the very first meal of the New Year round challot or loaves are used to indicate the unity of God. Just as a circle has no beginning nor end, so God is eternal. The shape also reminds one of a crown and the theme of the kingship of the Almighty recurs during the Festival.

Instead of salt being sprinkled over the challa, the bread is dipped into honey to express hope for a sweet and good year. Hebrew letters also have a numerical value. The numerical value of the word for honey, *dvash*, is 306 which is also the numerical

value of *av harachamim*, which means Father of Mercy.

As a first course it is customary to eat the head of a fish, with the brief prayer, 'May the coming year bring us to reach the head of society and not its tail.' The commentator Abudraham remarks that just as fish multiply rapidly, so should good deeds increase.

In the same way, pomegranates are eaten, in the hope that good deeds will be as many as the seeds of the pomegranate.

During the meal the traditional dish of *tzimmas*, made of carrots, sweet potatoes and honey, symbolizes prayers for a good year. Honey cake and honey biscuits also help to bring sweetness and joy into the solemnity of the occasion.

8. The shofar is blown as Romanian Jews observe Rosh Hashanah

THE MONTHS OF THE JEWISH YEAR

with the Festivals and Fast Days occurring in them

1 NISAN	30 days	15	PASSOVER day 1
		16	PASSOVER day 2
		17 *to* 20	Chol ha-Mo'ed
		21	PASSOVER day 7
		22	PASSOVER day 8
		27	Yom Ha' Shoah
2 IYYAR	29 days	5	Yom Ha'atzmaut
		18	Lag ba-Omer
		28	Yom Yerushalayim
3 SIVAN	30 days	6	SHAVUOT day 1
		7	SHAVUOT day 2
4 TAMMUZ	29 days	17	Fast of Tammuz
5 AV	30 days	9	Tish'ah B'-Av
6 ELUL	29 days		
7 TISHRI	30 days	1	ROSH HASHANAH day 1
		2	ROSH HASHANAH day 2
		3	Fast of Gedaliah
		10	YOM KIPPUR
		15	SUKKOT day 1
		16	SUKKOT day 2
		17 *to* 21	Chol ha-Mo'ed
		21	Hoshana Rabbah
		22	SHEMINI ATZERET
		23	SIMCHAT TORAH
8 CHESHVAN	29/30 days		
9 KISLEV	29/30 days	25 *to* 29/30	Chanukah days 1 *to* 5/6
10 TEVET	29 days	1 to 3/2	Chanukah days 6/7 to 8
		10	Fast of Tevet
11 SHEVAT	30 days	15	Tu B'Shevat
12 ADAR	29 days	14	Purim
ADAR RISHON	30 days		
13 ADAR SHENI	29 days	14	Purim

Yom Kippur

At the judgment on Rosh Hashanah, the completely righteous and absolute sinners are judged – everyone else is given a ten-day reprieve. It is a time to ask forgiveness of anyone whom one has wronged. This is necessary before God will grant pardon. If one has sinned against God, then repentance is necessary. Jews do not believe in original sin, but recognize that within each person there is a good and evil inclination (*yetzer tov* and *yetzer ha-ra*). The true sacrifice on the Day of Atonement, Yom Kippur, is a humble heart.

This solemn absolution of vows and promises refers only to those vows which a person may have voluntarily promised to the Almighty . . . it does not in the least possible degree affect the promises or obligations entered into between man and man, as the latter can only be dissolved by the mutual consent of the parties.

From the Sephardi or Spanish Prayer book

People sometimes ask Jews if they are able to forgive what the Nazis did during the Holocaust. Jews say that they cannot speak on behalf of those who were murdered – they cannot pronounce forgiveness on behalf of others. There are subtle but significant differences in Jewish and Christian teaching about forgiveness.

Outward actions should indicate and reinforce this inner penitence. On Yom Kippur, Jews abstain from food and drink and sexual relations, but the day is not a sad one. The fast is a physical expression of repentance. It prevents any distraction during the day of prayer. Like the angels, Jews are not to be diverted from the service of God.

On the eve of Yom Kippur, the whole community – men, women and children – gather in the synagogue. (Sometimes synagogues are too small and special halls have to be used.) The men put on their prayer shawls, which are not normally worn at night and *kittels*, which are snow-white robes reflecting the purity of the day.

As night falls, the cantor begins to chant the words *Kol Nidre*, which are the opening words of the service on the eve of Yom Kippur. They signify the absolution of past vows to God which have not been kept and the intention to avoid future failure. To violate an oath is one of the worst of sins. The *Kol Nidre* is chanted three times, each time in a louder voice.

Kol Nidre

May we be absolved from all the vows and obligations we make to God in vain, from this Yom Kippur to the next – may it come to us for good; the duties and promises we cannot keep, the commitments and undertakings which should never have been made.

We ask to be forgiven and released from our own failings. Though all the promises of our fellowmen stand, may God annul the empty promises we made in our foolishness to Him alone, and shield us from their consequences.

Do not hold us to vows like these!
Do not hold us to obligations like these!
Do not hold us to such empty oaths.

It is a long service – but there is no reason to hurry home. The whole day has a single purpose: 'The attainment of the supreme blessing of at-one-ment – reconciliation with God'.

In the morning, worship is resumed and continues without a pause until nightfall – although some members of the congregation may go out for a breath of fresh air.

The morning service is followed by a reading of the Torah, which tells how the Yom Kippur service was observed in the ancient Temple (Lev. 16). After this, there is an additional service, called the *musaf*, which recalls the duties of the High Priest on the Day of Atonement, which was the one day when he entered the Holy of Holies in the Temple. Just as he repeatedly purified himself, so the worshipper repeatedly confesses his sins.

During the afternoon service, chapter 18 of Leviticus is read. The book of Jonah is also read. This proclaims God's longing for repentance, not only by Jews, but by all people, represented by the Ninevites. The book is a reminder that change of conduct is the true test of repentance. The Mishnah points out that it does not say 'God saw their sackcloth and their fasting' but that He 'saw what they did, how they had turned from their evil way' (Jonah 3.10).

Sukkot

Five days after the Day of Atonement, the festival of Tabernacles or Sukkot is celebrated (Lev. 23.34–36). The mood changes from repentance to the 'season of our gladness'.

Sukkot lasts for nine days. Traditionally, the first two and last two days are major festival days.

During the festival, Jews build temporary booths or tabernacles (hence the name of the festival) to remind themselves of the shelters in which they lived during the forty years in the wilderness (Lev. 23). It is the third of the festivals which recall the Exodus. The other two festivals, as we have seen, are Passover, when Israel escaped from Egypt and Shavuot, when God made a covenant with the children of Israel on Mount Sinai.

The booth or sukkah is lavishly decorated, especially with fruit. Sukkot is also a harvest festival.

Observant Jews build their own sukkah and eat their meals in it and perhaps sleep in it. Adjustments may be made because of lack of space or because of the weather. Most synagogues will make a communal sukkah. It is a time for hospitality.

Four species are used in the celebration of Sukkot (Lev. 23.40).

The fruit of a goodly tree is a citron, the etrog;
The palm branch is known as the lulav;
The myrtle is called the hadasah;
The willow is known as the aravah.

The last days of Sukkot have special names. The seventh day is *Hoshana Rabbah* – 'the great hosanna' – and the eighth is *Shemini Atzert*.

The ninth day of Sukkot is *Simchat Torah* or 'Rejoicing in the Law', which marks the completion of the cycle of Torah readings. The last chapter from Deuteronomy is read and immediately the cycle recommences, with a reading of the first chapter of Genesis. It is a night for dancing and singing.

9. Sukkot is celebrated in an English garden

Minor festivals

Life now returns to its normal rhythm, with only 'minor festivals' (i.e. ones that do not involve abstention from work) to interrupt it.

Chanukah

Late November or December sees the festival of Chanukah, which begins on the 25th Kislev and lasts for eight days. The customs of Chanukah – the lighting of the chanukiah, or nine branched candlestick, playing dreidel and eating potato latkes – are quite well known. The story of how the menorah or candelabrum in the Temple stayed alight for eight days is also quite familiar. The background to that story is not so well known, but it introduces us to an important period in Jewish history and is retold

10. A Chanukah Menorah

by Jews as a warning of the dangers of assimilation.

In 336 BCE, Alexander the Great conquered the Persian Empire, which included Judaea. After Alexander's death, his empire was divided. At first Judaea came under the control of the Ptolemies of Egypt. Many Jews now became influenced by Hellenistic ideas.

So as to understand Judaism better, King Ptolemy (285–246) arranged for the Bible to be translated into Greek – the version usually known as the Septuagint (sometimes indicated by the abbreviation LXX). Tradition says that 72 people were involved in the translation.

After a time the Seleucid Empire of Syria fought a long and bitter struggle to gain control over Judaea, which was a strategic link between Africa and Asia. Some Jews now assimilated to Greek fashions and beliefs. For example they wanted to take part in athletics. This involved being naked and some people wished to disguise their circumcision.

The ruler, Antiochus IV Epiphanes, was an unstable man. He was nicknamed Antiochus Epimanes, which means 'madman'. When he came to Jerusalem in 168 BCE, he plundered the Temple and took 10,000 captives. Then on 25th Kislev, he (a Gentile) entered the Temple, erected a statue of Zeus Olympus on the altar of burnt offerings and sacrificed a swine on it. He splattered the Holy of Holies with the pig's blood.

Antiochus wanted to destroy Jewish practice and culture. He prohibited Temple worship, forced Jews to desecrate the Sabbath and forbade circumcision. Led by Mattathias, some Jews rebelled. Antiochus mobilized his army to attack them, but – one of the miracles of Chanukah – the rebels led by Judah Maccabee (Judas Maccabaeus), one of the sons of Mattathias, managed to defeat the Greeks and capture Jerusalem.

The Temple was restored and thoroughly cleansed. Exactly three years to the day since it had been defiled by Antiochus, it was rededicated. When the time came to light the menorah, only one small jar of olive oil, which had not been defiled by the Greeks, could be found. It would be an eight day trip to get new pure oil, but the High Priest went ahead and lit the menorah. The oil lasted for eight days, until the new supply arrived. Next year, the leaders of Israel ordered that on every 25th of Kislev, the Jews should celebrate the miracle of Chanukah – the word which means dedication. (The story is told in the books of Maccabees.)

Jewish independence was not to last for long – as gradually the area came under Roman control, although, especially under King Herod the Great (37–4 BCE), the Jews had some autonomy. It is worth remembering that the majority of Jews now lived outside Israel, in what was known as the Diaspora, or dispersion.

In earliest times, the Chanukah menorahs were merely small individual clay lamps. On each night of Chanukah another lamp was added. Then large circular lamps with eight openings were made. Originally the Chanukah lamps would be put outside on the left of the doorpost opposite the mezuzah, which is a small container with words of the Bible inside, which is attached to the doorpost of Jewish homes. Because of persecution, the rabbis allowed the lights to be kindled indoors. Now as the lights did not have to contend with the elements, people began to make increasingly elaborate candelabras.

The candles are lit at night just after dark. One candle on the first night and another candle each night thereafter for eight nights in all. As one faces the menorah, the candles are inserted from right to left. An additional candle, called the *shamash*, or servant candle, is usually placed off to the side. The lighting of the candles with the *shamash* proceeds from left to right, starting with the candle for the newest night. The blessings are then recited, followed by the singing of a traditional song known as *Ma'oz Tzur*.

Purim

Chanukah commemorates an unsuccessful attempt to destroy the Jewish way of life. Purim recalls an attempt to destroy the Jewish people and is a thanksgiving to God for saving them from the threat of extermination nearly twenty-five centuries ago. The horrors of the Holocaust have given added poignancy to the commemoration.

Purim is a turnabout from 'anguish to joy, from mourning to festivity' (Esth. 9.22). It can be a boisterous festival. The story is in the Book of Esther.

In 586 BCE the first Temple was destroyed and the Jews living in the Holy Land were taken into exile in Babylon (now Iraq). About fifty years later the Persians, under Cyrus (*c.* 590–529 BCE), conquered Babylon (Isa. 45.1). The Jews were given permission to return to their homeland and to start rebuilding the Temple. This is recounted in the books of Ezra and Nehemiah.

In 481, Xerxes I (called Ahasuerus in the Bible) came to the throne. After a quarrel, Xerxes banished his wife, Vashti. A Jewish girl, Esther, was chosen to replace her. Her uncle Mordecai discovered a plot to assassinate the king. As a result some Persian nobles fell from favour and Xerxes appointed Haman, a foreigner, as his Prime Minister. He was one of the 'Troublers of Judah and Benjamin' and wanted to use his power to destroy the Jews completely. He found the excuse he wanted when Mordecai refused to bow to him.

Haman accused the Jews of disobeying the laws of Persia and obtained the king's consent to kill them. He was a superstitious man and cast lots (*purim* in the Assyrian language) to choose an auspicious day for the slaughter.

Mordecai told Esther about the plot and asked her to tell the king. But there was a difficulty. Anyone who appeared before the king without being summoned by him risked the death penalty, unless the king extended his golden sceptre. Eventually Esther agreed and asked all Jews to fast for three days on her behalf.

Esther, dressed in her most royal garb, entered the king's presence. He extended his golden sceptre to her and enquired what she wanted. She invited the king and Haman to a banquet. Haman left the banquet full of his own importance, but on the way home saw Mordecai. This filled him with anger. His wife advised him to build a gallows fifty cubits high on which to hang Mordecai.

That night, the king could not sleep. He asked his servants to read to him from the court chronicles. In them Xerxes discovered that Mordecai had never been rewarded for saving him from the plot to assassinate him. When Haman appeared at court, the king asked him 'What should be done for the man whom the king wishes to reward?' Haman thinking that it was he and not Mordecai who was to be rewarded, said that the man to be honoured should be dressed in royal clothing, ride upon a royal horse and be led through the city streets by a herald. The King then told Haman to arrange this for Mordecai!

At a second banquet, Esther revealed to the king the plot to destroy her people. The king then ordered Haman's execution and elevated Mordecai to a position of influence.

The day before Purim is a fast, called the fast of Esther. Before the afternoon service, there is a special charity collection, which is called *machazit hashekel* (the value of a half shekel). This commemorates the tax which all Jews used to pay towards the upkeep of the Temple.

At nightfall the festival of Purim begins. People come to the synagogue dressed in their Sabbath clothes. During the service the book of Esther is read.

The book is called the Megillah or scroll. It is read from a scroll of parchment. Sometimes, before it is read, it is unrolled and folded over on itself several times so that it resembles a letter. This is because the Scroll of Esther mentions 'because of all the words of this letter' and because this is how royal proclamations were read in the Persian Empire.

During the reading of the scroll, whenever Haman's name is mentioned, the children jeer, stamp their feet and even use football rattles. (For a time, some modern Jews thought the ceremonies unedifying and that they appeared to sanction revenge, so they did not observe Purim, but the Festival has regained popularity amongst all sections of Jews.)

After the service, people go home to a special meal. People are encouraged to drink plenty of wine – until they cannot tell the difference between the numerical value of the Hebrew words for 'cursed is Haman' and 'blessed is Mordecai'. One explanation is that this is a reminder of the fact that Xerxes exiled his first queen, Vashti, because he

11. Children enjoy Purim

was drunk and it was this that made it possible for Esther to become queen. Other explanations stress the need to believe in God's providence. Even when a person is confused or made drowsy by too much wine, God protects him.

It is also a time to collect for charities. To ensure that everyone has enough food for Purim, people send gifts of food to their friends. Children are fully involved and dress up and act out the characters in the story. There are special foods. The *Hamantshen* resemble the three-cornered hat that Haman wore. Poppy seeds are also used in several recipes. The German word for poppy, *mohn*, sounds like Haman.

Next day, at the synagogue, the scroll is read for a second time. The day following is called Shushan Purim, to remember the people of Shushan who did not overcome their enemies until the second day.

Fast days

Besides Yom Kippur, the following days, which take their names from the day of the month on which they fall, are kept as fast days:

The Tenth day of Tevet commemorates the day when Nebuchadnezzar laid siege to Jerusalem. He eventually captured Jerusalem and forced the Jews into exile.

The Seventeenth day of Tammuz recalls the breaching of the walls of Jerusalem by the Babylonians and, centuries later, by the Romans.

The Ninth day of Av, called Tish'ah B'-Av, commemorates the first and second destructions of the Temple (in 586 BCE and 70 CE). It is also a day on which other tragic events are recalled, such as the expulsion of the Jews from England in 1290 and from Spain in 1492. Some synagogues also recall the victims of the Holocaust.

The Third day of Tishri, which is the Fast of Gedaliah, marks the assassination of Gedaliah who was friendly to Nehemiah's efforts to restore Jerusalem.

The days before Purim and Pesach are also fasts.

The first is a reminder of Esther's fast. The second, by first born only, is an act of identification with the sufferings of the Egyptians.

Other special days

Holocaust Day: Yom Ha'Shoah

Although victims of the Holocaust may be remembered at Tish'ah B'-Av, there is increasing observance of Holocaust Day or Yom Ha'Shoah, on the Twenty-seventh day of the month of Nisan. This is the date which was proclaimed as Holocaust Remembrance Day in Israel by the Knesset in 1951. The day was chosen as it is close to the end of the Warsaw Ghetto Uprising and because it occurs during the traditional mourning period of the Counting of the Omer.

The term 'holocaust' is theological in origin rather than historical. It is an English derivative from the Greek translation of the Hebrew *olah*, which means a sacrificial offering burnt whole before the Lord. Some think the word already softens the horror of what happened by importing a religious meaning. Also the word is used of many horrendous events, so can mask the uniqueness of what happened to the Jews under the Nazis.

The Hebrew (and also Yiddish) word *Churban*, meaning destruction, is more stark and refers to the results of the event itself. The word, however, is already used in rabbinic literature of the destruction of the first and second Temples. The Hebrew word *Shoah*, which also means destruction, is free from both historical and theological associations.

Israel Independence Day: Yom Ha'atzmaut

Israel Independence Day, Yom Ha'atzmaut, is really a secular commemoration, although special services may be held on that day. On Mount Herzl in Jerusalem there is a memorial service for those who died fighting for Israel. Twelve great flames are lit.

After the destruction of Jerusalem in 70 CE, for nearly two thousand years, Jews lived in dispersion and had no country of their own. Even so, through the centuries a few Jews continued to live in the Holy Land. Towards the end of the last century Theodor Herzl, aware of the continuing threat of antisemitism, wrote *Der Judenstaat* (1894), which called for the creation of a Jewish state. In 1897 the first Zionist Congress met to try to bring this about. 'If you wish it,' Herzl said, 'it is not a dream to live as a free people in your own land.' He predicted that a Jewish state would be in existence within fifty years. In November 1947, the United Nations agreed to the establishment of the State of Israel and on 14 May 1948 Ben Gurion proclaimed the State of Israel.

The New Year for Trees: Tu B'Shevat

The New Year for Trees, which is observed on the fifteenth day of the month of Shevat, has become a popular festival. There are other new years in the Jewish calendar, but this is a special one for trees. In Leviticus 19 there is the verse, 'And when you come into the land and have planted trees, you shall count the fruit as forbidden for three years; . . . In the fourth year, the fruit shall be holy, for giving praise to God, but in the fifth year you may eat the fruit.' On this special day Jews all over the world plant trees. There has been widespread re-afforestation in Israel in recent years and the festival reminds people of the need to care for the environment.

4

The Home and the Sabbath

A miniature sanctuary

The home

The Jewish home is considered a miniature sanctuary. This is shown both by some of the objects in a Jewish home and by traditional practices: but most of all by a spirit of domestic harmony.

> 'He who loves his wife as much as himself honours her more than himself: he who rears children in the right manner, that man will have peace in his household.'
>
> 'A home where there is dissension will not last.'
>
> 'Hospitality is even more important and meritorious than greeting the glory of the Divine Presence.'
>
> Rabbinic sayings

The Pharisees believed that all Jews were called to be a holy people, not just the priests. They were concerned for the sanctification of the whole of life. They and the rabbis after them have recognized the importance of the home in strengthening Jewish faith and identity.

A Jewish home is likely to have a number of distinctive objects, such as a menorah or candelabrum, books about Israel, perhaps a card wishing the son of the family well on his Barmitzvah when he becomes an adult member of the house of Israel, candles for the Sabbath, a mezuzah on the doorpost as well as special clothes such as a prayer shawl and the head covering or *kippah* that the male members of the family may wear.

Mezuzah

When a Jewish family moves into a new home, one of the first things brought in, as a reminder of the Temple and the altar, is bread and salt.

Quite soon a dedication ceremony is arranged. This begins with the fixing of a mezuzah, in a sloping position, on the top third of the right doorpost of the entrance and sometimes of each doorway of the house.

Whilst the mezuzah is fixed, a blessing is recited: 'Blessed art thou, O Lord our God, King of the universe, who hast sanctified us by the commandments, and commanded us to affix the mezuzah.'

> 'And these words which I command you this day shall be upon your heart . . . and you shall write upon the doorposts of your houses and upon your gates.'
>
> (Deut. 6.9)

A mezuzah is a parchment scroll bearing two passages from the Bible. These are the first two paragraphs of what is called the Shema, from the word 'hear' in 'Hear O Israel . . .' (See Deut. 6.4–9 and 11.13–21). These verses declare the Oneness of God and the covenant relationship between God and the Jewish people.

A mezuzah must be handwritten by a trained scribe on parchment. Before starting to write, the scribe cuts the parchment into a square. He then scores lines lightly across to make sure that the writing will be straight. The words should be written on twenty-two lines, corresponding to the number of letters in the Hebrew alphabet.

The scroll is normally put into a protective case. Every seven years it should be checked to ensure that the writing is legible.

Synagogues sometimes present a couple when they get married with a mezuzah for the new home.

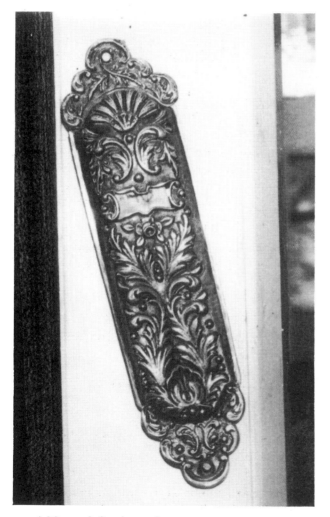

12. A Mezuzah fixed on a doorpost

Special clothes

'These words shall be upon your heart.' Clothes too can be a reminder of God. It was probably during Pharisaic times that Jewish men started to wear *tefillin*, which are a pair of cubical leather boxes containing four scriptural texts handwritten on parchment. The texts are: Deut. 6.4–9; and usually Ex. 13.1–10; 11–16 and Deut. 11.13–21.

One of the boxes is tied on the left upper arm, opposite the heart and its strap wound seven times round the forearm, then round the middle finger and the palm of the hand. The other box is placed on the forehead, with its two straps knotted together above the nape of the neck, then brought forward over the shoulders.

Tefillin are worn by observant male Jews during morning prayers every day except sabbaths and festivals.

During morning prayers Jewish males also wear the *tallit*, or prayer robe. This is a four-cornered square or rectangle of cloth, usually made of wool or silk. Attached to each of the corners are fringes, known as *tzizit*.

The tallit or prayer robe needs to be distinguished from the *tallit katan* that a Jewish male may put on when he gets dressed and wear as an undergarment. It again is a four cornered garment, with a hole for the head and with fringes, which is worn throughout the day every day.

> 'They shall make for themselves fringes on the corners of their garments . . . and you shall see them and remember all the commandments of the Lord.'
> (Num. 15.38–9)

Observant Jewish males also wear a *kippah*, sometimes called a *kupple*, which is a small cap. This is worn as a sign of respect for God. Some Jews wear a kippah at all times, others may only wear one for times of prayer or when they go to a synagogue.

Married women also, traditionally, cover their heads as a sign of modesty.

13. A young Jew wearing tefillin and a tallit

kosher rules is that milk and meatfoods must not come in contact with each other.

There are also rules about what food may or may not be eaten. If food is kosher, a Jew is allowed to eat it. If it is not allowed it is called trefah. Most of the food laws come in Leviticus 11 or Deuteronomy 14, but they have been elaborated over the centuries by rabbinic discussion. Progressive Jews reject some of these elaborations.

Insects are not allowed, although all vegetables are allowed. Vegetables need, therefore, to be carefully washed to make sure there are no insects on them.

Chicken, turkey, duck and goose are regarded as kosher. Fish, to be kosher, must have both fins and scales. Animals to be kosher must chew the cud and have cloven hooves. Pigs are the most common animals which many other people eat but which are not kosher.

Approved methods of slaughter are carefully defined. The method of killing by a single stroke across the neck with a very sharp knife is called shechita. The Torah commands Jews not to eat the blood of animals and birds. By salting and draining care is taken to remove the blood before the meat is cooked.

Although these rules may have hygienic benefits, they are obeyed because they are God's commands.

Kosher

Another way of showing that the home is a sanctuary is by the observance of kashrut, or the keeping of kosher. The term kashrut denotes the totality of Jewish food laws, their maintenance, observance and supervision by the rabbinic authorities. Kosher denotes all that is free for human consumption according to these rules.

In the kitchen of an Orthodox Jewish home, you are likely to find separate sets of crockery, cutlery and utensils for meat and for dairy products. They are washed up separately. This is because one of the

---

A Sample Menu for a Sabbath (Friday) evening

Chicken soup with matzo balls
Roast chicken and vegetables
Kugel (a pudding based on egg noodles)
Lemon tea (no milk, because this is a meat meal)

A Sample Menu for a Sabbath (Saturday) lunch

Cold fried fish
Fruit Salad

This is a cold meal because of restrictions on preparing or heating meals on the Sabbath.

The Sabbath

'Six days you shall do your work, but on the seventh day you shall rest' (Ex. 23.12).

'More than the Jews have kept the Sabbath, the Sabbath has kept the Jews' said the modern Jewish thinker, Achad Ha-am. It has helped Jews preserve their identity and given them courage during repeated persecution. It has strengthened family ties. Much of the Sabbath observance is at home. This again shows the importance of the home in Jewish life.

We shall think about the Sabbath in four ways. First we shall listen to what some Jews feel about the Sabbath. Then we shall find out what happens on the Sabbath, then see how the rabbis decided what was work and then consider the deeper meanings of the Sabbath.

Many people consider the idea of keeping strictly a day of rest unattractive and think it would be boring and repressive. Jewish writers stress the value of the practice.

Jewish feelings about the Sabbath

Rab Abraham Guigui has described what happened in Morocco where he grew up between the two World Wars. 'Generally speaking, above all in Morocco, the Jews worked terribly hard during the week. They were worried about practical matters, they weren't rich; their neighbours weren't always friendly. They had all kinds of disasters to cope with . . . But when the sabbath came, all their cares, all their problems vanished. For the Jew, especially those in Morocco, the sabbath is in a sense an oasis in time, a moment when all these tribulations disappear and they enter a different atmosphere, a different world, a different time. That is why the sabbath is so important in Jewish tradition and liturgy . . . The father of the house would always have an eye on the sabbath and deny himself all sorts of things during the week so as to be able to buy only the best for the sabbath. The wife makes an extra effort to give the house a festive air, to make everything glitter and shine. This whole atmosphere . . . makes the sabbath a haven of peace, a moment of rest and relaxation, a delight for the Jew' (personal interview in Willem Zuidema, *God's Partner*, SCM Press 1987, pp. 76–7).

The British Reform rabbi Jonathan Romain has written: 'The Sabbath's theme of rest – physical and spiritual – is as relevant in today's world of intense pressure as it was in ancient times of strenuous labour. Technology and increased leisure time have brought many benefits but they often mean that we do more rather than less. In addition, they do not address the question of one's inner calm, and they have not lessened the need for personal renewal' (*Faith and Practice*, Reform Synagogues of Great Britain 1991, p. 130).

What happens on the Sabbath?

The command to keep the Sabbath is given in Exodus 20.8 and Deuteronomy 5.12. There is a rabbinic comment that two different words are used – 'remember' and 'observe' – as a reminder that the Sabbath is kept in both positive and negative ways. Ceasing from work allows time to think about God, to be with one's family and to be spiritually and physically refreshed.

Sabbath rest cannot just happen without a lot of preparation. Responsibilities at work should be dealt with, all shopping completed, the home cleaned, special meals prepared for Friday evening and Saturday lunch and the table laid with Sabbath requirements and adornments. These include the white table cloth, two candlesticks and candles, two *challot* or braided loaves covered by a cloth, salt, wine and fresh flowers.

Members of the family will have prepared by having a bath or shower and putting on clean clothes.

The Sabbath is welcomed on Friday evening both at home and in the synagogue. In the synagogue, the service includes a number of psalms. It ends with the Yigdal, a hymn of praise to God and a blessing.

At home the Sabbath is welcomed by the lighting

of candles by the woman of the house. She then covers her eyes and recites a blessing: 'Blessed are You, O Lord our God, King of the Universe, who have hallowed us by Your commandments and commanded us to kindle Sabbath lights.'

The father then blesses any children and reads a passage praising the woman of the house (Prov. 31.10–31).

The meal is preceded by the making of *kiddush* – the saying of a blessing – over the bread and wine. Then everyone greets each other with the traditional greeting, *Shabbat Shalom*, 'A Peaceful Sabbath'. The meal itself is a special and relaxed meal, followed by songs, *zemirot*, stories and conversation.

Shabbat morning, traditionally, is spent in the synagogue. Then after another family meal the day is spent in study of Torah or in relaxation. There is a saying that 'sleep on the Sabbath is a real enjoyment'.

When dusk falls it is time to say goodbye to the 'Sabbath Queen' with the simple ceremony of Havdalah. The woman of the house chants a prayer thanking God for the gift of the sabbath and seeking health and happiness for her family and for the Jewish people. A blessing is said over the wine: 'May the joy of the Sabbath brighten the coming week.' A small box of sweet-smelling spices is passed round. The family breathes in the scent from the spices, remembering the incense used in the Temple services and hoping that the coming week will be a sweet and good one. The youngest member of the family often holds a special braided candle. The candle represents the light of the sabbath brightening the coming week. A blessing is said over the candle as a reminder that light was the first thing God created.

What work is forbidden on the Sabbath?

There is today, as there has been since at least rabbinic times, considerable discussion about what counts as work and is therefore not permitted on a Sabbath. The arguments of Jesus with the Pharisees, as reported in the New Testament, have the character of such rabbinic debates.

Whilst all agreed that the saving of life had priority over Sabbath rules, the rabbinic texts show different rulings on whether it was allowed to set a broken limb on the Sabbath. In the rabbinic commentary, known as the Mishnah, it was thought that no harm would be caused by waiting. Setting a broken limb was considered to come under the category of 'building'. The rabbis of the Talmud rejected this particular ruling, and allowed setting a fracture on the Sabbath.

Today, Progressive Jews have relaxed some of the traditional rules. Each family makes its own decisions and maybe different members of the family themselves disagree about whether gardening is work or a relaxing hobby or whether watching television or using the telephone is permitted.

People sometimes think that using modern technology – such as time switches or automatic ovens – is a way of getting round the rules. But this is a mistake. The intention of the rules was positive: to ensure freedom from work.

The meaning of Sabbath observance

It is easy to be fascinated by the special and beautiful *Shabbat* ceremonies. It is important also to reflect on the meaning of the Sabbath and its importance in Jewish life. Jewish teachers have emphasized various aspects of the Sabbath's significance.

The Hallowing of time. Abraham J. Heschel (1907–1972), a great American Jewish thinker, called the Sabbath 'a palace or sanctuary in time'. Judaism has not given the world any great buildings, such as the pyramids or the cathedrals. Its monuments are the Bible and the Sabbath.

Heschel wrote: 'Judaism is a religion of history, a religion of time. The God of Israel was not primarily to be found in the facts of nature. He spoke through events in history. While the deities of other peoples were associated with places or things, the God of the prophets was a God of events: the Redeemer from slavery, the Revealer of the Torah. He manifests Himself in events of history rather than in things or places' (A. J.Heschel, *God in Search of Man*, Harper and Row, New York 1966, p. 200).

God's sovereignty over nature. Many early civilizations virtually identified the divine with nature. By resting after the work of creation God affirmed his sovereignty over nature. Men and women by sharing in God's day of rest are set apart from the other creatures.

Human dignity is affirmed and efforts to reduce people to beasts of burden are resisted. The Sabbath is a liberating and humanizing institution.

The Sabbath rest is extended to the animal creation and so is a check on exploitation and teaches reverence for the natural world.

The Sabbath has strengthened Jewish identity. In times of dispersion and exile Jews have affirmed their identity by keeping the Sabbath. Sabbath observance was forbidden by Antiochus Epiphanes in the second century BCE. The Inquisition tortured those Jews, known as Marranos, who had forcibly converted to Christianity and who were suspected of still secretly observing the Sabbath.

The Sabbath strengthens Jewish family life. Where possible, the whole family gets together for the Sabbath and spends time together. The way the Sabbath is observed also shows the importance of the home in Jewish religious life. People who would be by themselves are often invited to join a family for the Sabbath.

The Sabbath is a time for study of the Torah and may encourage mystical contemplation. Genesis declares the Sabbath to be a divine as well as human rest day. The Sabbath becomes, therefore, in the words of the Liberal rabbi John Rayner, 'a contemplation of nature and its divine Creator, a listening to the heartbeat of the cosmos, a devotional exercise and a spiritual experience' (David J. Goldberg and John Rayner, *The Jewish People*, Penguin 1989, p. 340).

14. The special Sabbath loaves are shared at the kiddush

5

Rites of Passage

'Five is the age for starting to study scripture, . . . thirteen is the age for observing the commandments, eighteen for marriage . . .'

Each day, for an Orthodox Jew, there are many reminders of God's presence. Major events in each person's own life are also marked by special ceremonies, which are often called rites of passage.

Circumcision

On the eighth day after his birth a Jewish baby boy is circumcised in a ceremony called in Hebrew *Brit milah*. Immediately after the circumcision, the father says, 'Blessed are you, O Lord our God, King of the Universe, who has made us holy by your commandments and has commanded us to make our sons enter into the covenant of Abraham our Father.'

Circumcision affirms the child's membership of God's chosen people. It does not make a person a Jew. Any child of a Jewish mother is a Jew – even an uncircumcised Jew is, according to halakhah, still a Jew. If someone who does not have a Jewish mother wishes to convert to Judaism, a decision has to be made by the Beth Din or Rabbinic Court, following study and circumcision.

Circumcision has a long history and was practised by other peoples of the Ancient Near East. It is still sometimes practised for medical reasons: but for Jews it is a sign in the flesh of their relationship with God.

A circumcision is a happy event. Children are regarded as a great blessing. They assure the continuity of the Jewish people which at different times in history has been endangered by persecution. There may be a ceremony of 'Welcome to the Male Child' either on the night following the child's birth or on the night before the circumcision.

The circumcision may be performed in hospital, before the mother and baby leave to go home. Usually the ceremony is at home or in the synagogue. It takes place on the eighth day, even if this is a sabbath or the Day of Atonement. The fact that circumcision takes precedence over all other special events and festivals indicates how important it is.

Circumcision is carried out by a carefully trained man called a mohel. When the mohel is ready, one of the women takes the child from his mother and carries him, on a cushion, to the room where the men are gathered. There she hands the infant to her husband who carries him to the mohel. Before performing the circumcision, the mohel will place the child briefly on an empty chair known as the Chair of Elijah. There is an ancient belief that the spirit of the prophet Elijah visits every circumcision.

The child is placed on the lap of the man chosen by the father to be his companion, who is called a sandek. It is considered a great honour to be asked to be the sandek. The mohel snips the foreskin of the penis, removes the inner lining and puts on a

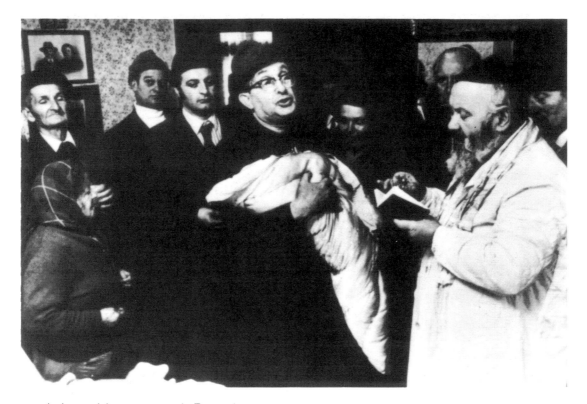

15. A circumcision ceremony in Romania

dressing to stop the bleeding. The father then recites the blessing already quoted and the mohel will hold the child and bless and name him. The child is handed back to the man who brought him in and in turn to his wife who returns the child to his mother, who will probably feed him.

There follows a festive meal to celebrate the entry of a new Jewish soul into the 'Covenant of Father Abraham'.

Whilst a boy is named at his circumcision, a girl is usually named on the first or fourth Sabbath after her birth during the synagogue service. Again there is probably a celebration meal afterwards.

Jews did not have family names until required to do so by some European governments in the eighteenth and nineteenth centuries. Many Jews simply adopted their fathers' first names as their surnames, for example Abrams, Jacobs or Samuel-son. Some names indicate the place of origin or the family's occupation. The name Cohen indicates priestly descent and Levy indicates descent from the tribe of Levi. Even if Jews have secular names, they usually also have a Jewish, normally a Hebrew name. There are various traditions about how to choose a name. It may be after a deceased relative to perpetuate their memory or it may be a way of honouring a living relation. The Hebrew name may be the Hebrew translation of, or nearest sound-equivalent to, the English forename.

'Hear, O Israel, the Lord is our God, the Lord is One.' One tradition says that the first words a child should be taught to say are the *Shema*.

16. A Batmitzvah in a progressive synagogue

Barmitzvah and Batmitzvah

Jews have always put great stress on education. It is a duty of the father not only to have his son circumcised, but also to teach him the Law or Torah and a trade. Some sources say he should teach his child to swim and civic responsibilities, as well.

The teaching of Torah, that is religious education, receives great emphasis. It includes learning to read Hebrew. If children attend Jewish schools, they will learn about their heritage there. Otherwise, they will learn by attending classes at the synagogue, which all Jewish children are encouraged to attend.

The age of majority was fixed by the rabbis, in relation to the onset of puberty, at thirteen for boys and twelve for girls. The first records of a coming-of-age ceremony, now called barmitzvah, date to the Middle Ages.

The central feature of the ceremony is for the boy to exercise his newly-acquired status as an adult member of the community by reading part of the Torah section for the sabbath, or at least a blessing on the Torah. This, of course, requires preparation and instruction. Normally also the rabbi will ensure that the boy knows how to use tefillin.

After his son has read his portion, the father

recites a blessing thanking God for bringing his son to maturity.

The ceremony in the synagogue is often followed by a lavish party where the boy is given generous gifts.

In recent years Progressive Jews have started to observe for girls a similar ceremony, known as a batmitzvah. Some Orthodox Jews also now have a ceremony for girls, often called bat chayil. This may involve a group of girls reciting psalms or special readings.

17. Barmitzvahs are a time for cards and presents

Marriage

Marriage is highly esteemed in the Jewish tradition and was declared to be an obligation. Celibacy has never been highly regarded – and the Essene community at the Dead Sea was very unusual in being celibate. In ancient Judaism priests were not celibate and the High Priest was encouraged to marry (Lev. 21.13f.).

Jewish teaching about marriage

In Jewish teaching, marriage serves three purposes:

1. The propagation of the human species, to fulfil the command 'be fruitful and multiply'. According to Talmudic law, the requirement is fulfilled when a man has begotten at least one son and one daughter. Thereafter, Orthodox Jews allow contraception, although some ultra-Orthodox Jews even then view contraception with disfavour, unless the consequences of pregnancy would be life-threatening.

The method of contraception has to avoid the ban on a man spilling his seed (see Gen. 38.9–10). The pill, the diaphragm and spermicide are acceptable methods of contraception, because they do not interfere with the sexual act. The use of the condom is forbidden as it prevents the man's seed entering the womb. The inter-uterine device is acceptable, although it may cause infertility.

Vasectomy is forbidden as it is regarded as akin to castration, which is prohibited in Jewish law, although the sterilization of a woman is allowed.

Progressive Judaism leaves these matters to the couple to decide for themselves. For them the criterion for deciding about methods of birth control would be what method is the most reliable and best for the couple's health.

Jewish tradition allows abortion if the mother's life is in danger.

The foetus is not considered a human being until the head or the greater part of the body has emerged from the mother's womb.

> 'A man without a wife lives without blessing, life, joy, help, good and peace.'
>
> Rabbinic saying

2. The second reason for marriage is companionship. Marriage makes for happiness.

Marriage is often compared to God's eternal covenant with Israel (Hos. 2.19). It should be lifelong and divorce is regarded with sadness. Divorce is, however, allowed on the grounds of serious matrimonial offence or when all attempts at reconciliation have failed. The procedure, based on Deut. 24.1–4, takes place before a rabbinic court and involves the writing of a writ of divorce, called a *get* on behalf of the husband and its delivery to the wife, whose consent has been required since mediaeval times. In most countries today, Jews come under the civil law of the land where they live so they need first to obtain a civil divorce.

> 'The very altar weeps when a man divorces the wife of his youth.'
>
> Rabbinic saying, referring to Mal. 2.14ff.

3. Thirdly, marriage is highly regarded in Jewish tradition because it establishes the family as the basic social unit and the home as the 'little sanctuary' (Ezek. 11.16) in which the father is like a priest, the mother like a priestess, and the dining-room table like an altar. The family provides the setting in which children can enjoy their childhood and grow to maturity under the loving protection and guidance of their parents, and in which the Jewish religion can be practised, experienced and transmitted from generation to generation.

Although the importance of family life is stressed in Judaism, Jews cannot escape the pressures of modern life. The number of divorces has increased and a number of Jews 'marry out', that is to say they marry non-Jews. This is discouraged by rabbinic authorities and in Britain hardly any rabbis will take part in 'joint' services, although in the USA non-Orthodox rabbis may arrange a religious ceremony.

All the above may appear to have been written from a male standpoint and this reflects the tradition, which derives from a patriarchal society. Progressive Judaism, however, affirms the equality of the sexes, as shown for example in the fact that men and women sit together in the synagogue.

Traditional material affirms the dignity of women and also encourages the enjoyment of sex. A husband is told to have thought for his wife's pleasure during intercourse. Sexual relations before marriage are strictly forbidden.

The wedding

A wedding can take place on any day of the week except a sabbath or a festival. A few days before the wedding the bride will probably visit a mikveh, or immersion pool, to purify herself.

The concept of purification, to be found in other religions such as Hinduism, may be easily misunderstood. It dates back at least to the time of the Temple, when a person might be going there to present an offering. To approach the Temple a person had to be in a special state of purity, but it was easy in every-day life to be defiled – perhaps by touching a corpse or a dead animal or by being near a woman who was menstruating. Bathing was a way of purification, although the physical cleansing was symbolic of inner purification.

Since the destruction of the Temple, there has been little occasion for men to use a mikveh. Today the mikveh is mainly used by women, who immerse themselves before the wedding or after menstruation and childbirth. The custom had lapsed amongst all but the most Orthodox Jewish women, although today it has found favour amongst some women as a specifically feminist ritual. In Progressive Judaism, the use of the mikveh is entirely optional, except as one of the rites involved in conversion. In both Orthodox and Progressive Judaism, converts to Judaism are required to immerse themselves.

On the wedding day itself the couple fast until

the ceremony. This takes place under a chuppah or canopy, held on four poles, which may be decorated with flowers.

Although there are variations, a Jewish wedding takes a set form:

Initial blessings of wine and of the marriage.
The ring.
The marriage contract.
The final (seven) blessings.

Originally the marriage ceremony was in two parts – the betrothal and the wedding – with about a year between them. The betrothal took place in the bride's home. The couple became legally bound to each other, but did not live together. The first part is now what is known as the initial blessings. A cup of wine is blessed as a symbol of joy. Both partners drink from it and share their joy.

The crucial moment now, as in the past, is after the bride has entered the chuppah to join the bridegroom and the relatives and the rabbi. The bridegroom places the ring on the bride's finger – traditionally this is the forefinger of the right hand where it can be most clearly displayed to witnesses. Later it is transferred to the 'wedding finger'.

The bridegroom says: 'Behold, you are consecrated to me by this ring according to the Law of Moses and of Israel.' The words are important both religiously and legally.

Then the officiant reads out the marriage contract or ketubah, which is in Aramaic. Often an English summary is read. It may be signed by the bride and groom. The contract makes clear the husband's responsibility to provide for his wife.

The ceremony concludes with further blessings, again over a cup of wine from which both partners drink. The seven blessings link the couple with the story of creation, the history of Israel and its future hopes.

The ceremony may include a sermon from the rabbi, singing and the breaking of a glass, which the groom steps on as a reminder of the destruction of the Temple and the couple's awareness that whilst they are happy, others may be sad. As the groom does this the guests wish the couple good luck with the traditional word *mazeltov*. After the ceremony, the couple will spend a short while together privately, as a time to relax and break their fast and to indicate their new status.

There are some differences in a Progressive Jewish wedding. With the emphasis on the equality of women, the bride may present her husband with a ring. She also makes a reciprocal vow, declaring in Hebrew, 'And you are married to me in holiness according to the Law of Moses and of Israel.' The ring is put straight on to the third finger of the left hand.

After their honeymoon, the couple return to their marital home, which is dedicated at a ceremony

18. A wedding takes place under a chuppah or canopy

called *chanukat ha'bayit* or 'consecration of the home'. The couple settle down to the rhythm of domestic life, including its daily, weekly, yearly and life-cycle religious observances.

Burial

Judaism encourages its adherents to accept the aging process and mortality. In the Torah, as in all traditional societies, respect for the elderly is encouraged.

When a person is dying, relatives seek to gather round him or her. The dying person or the relatives may want a rabbi to be present. If possible, a person's last moments should be spent in making a confession and in reciting the Shema.

Family and friends stay with a person during the moment of death. They then make sure the eyes and mouth are closed. Traditionally the body is left for about eight minutes while a feather is left over the mouth and nostrils, which are watched for any sign of breathing. Those present will bless God as the true judge and make a short tear in their clothes as a sign of grief.

If no Jews are present, it is permitted for non-Jewish members of the hospital staff to carry out the following: Close the eyes; tie up the jaw; keep the arms and hands straight and remove any tubes or instruments. The corpse should then be wrapped in a plain sheet without religious emblems, and placed in the mortuary or other special room for Jewish bodies.

Some Orthodox Jews may object to post-mortem examinations, unless required by law. They may also be hesitant about the giving of organs for transplant use, because of the biblical injunction not to mutilate the body. As soon as the doctor has issued a death certificate, members of the burial society, *Chevra Kaddisha*, will prepare the body for burial by washing it thoroughly. The body is wrapped in a plain linen shroud and a male is usually buried wearing the tallit in which he prayed during his lifetime. Once the body is ready, it is placed in a simple, unpolished wooden box with no brass handles or internal padding. In death, rich and poor are treated alike.

The funeral which, if possible, takes place within twenty-four hours of death, is a simple affair. Some psalms are read, followed by a short prayer praising God for granting life and accepting that it has been taken away. A rabbi may give a talk about the dead person.

After the coffin is lowered into the ground, earth is heaped on it or stones. Friends offer words of comfort to the mourner. The traditional greeting is to wish the mourner a long life. This may seem strange, but affirms the Jewish sense of the goodness of life and that mourners still have their future ahead of them. Everyone washes their hands before leaving the cemetry, which is known euphemistically as *beit olam*, the 'house of eternity', or *beit chayyim*, the 'house of the living'.

Orthodox Judaism does not allow cremation, but this is permitted by Progressive Jews.

Mourning

Between death and the burial the mourner, called *onen*, is exempt from normal religious observances. After the burial, the mourner, now called an *aval*, observes an intense period of mourning for seven days – usually called shiv'ah, which means seven. During this week the mourners usually gather in one of their homes and should not leave it unless absolutely necessary. Friends and fellow members of the synagogue visit regularly and bring food. Three times a day they will pray with the mourners, who recite the memorial prayer or kaddish, which is not a prayer for the dead, but a declaration of God's greatness and a prayer for the coming age of universal peace.

At the end of the week people leave the house and resume their daily tasks, but the official period of mourning continues for a year – more strictly for the first month and to a lesser extent thereafter, for instance saying the kaddish each day for eleven months.

On the anniversary of the death, known by its

Yiddish name *yarhzeit*, a candle is kept burning through the day and the night and kaddish is again said. For as long as the immediate relatives live, they will light a candle and say kaddish on each *yarhzeit*.

Often the anniversary is chosen as the time to put a headstone over the grave. Sephardi graves are usually flat and Ashkenazi upright.

Some of the rituals may appear complicated and not all Jews observe them in full. It is, however, increasingly appreciated that these rites play a therapeutic role in helping the mourners, with the support of their community, to cope with their grief and gradually to surmount it.

Resurrection

Belief in an afterlife has been an integral part of Jewish belief for over two thousand years, although there are few references to this in the Hebrew Bible. By the Maccabean age, belief in life after death had gained official recognition. The belief took two forms. One was belief in the bodily resurrection of the dead (see Dan. 12.2 and II Macc. 7.9) in the Messianic age. The other was belief in the survival of the soul (see Wisd. 3.1–4).

By the first century CE, the Pharisees, unlike the Sadducees, accepted both doctrines. As a result the liturgy of the synagogue both asserts that God 'revives the dead' and that he has 'implanted eternal life within us'. There is some variety in Jewish thinking about life after death and various images are used without great precision. God is often spoken of as judge, but ideas of heaven and hell were never developed in detail, as they were in mediaeval Christianity. Despite the vagueness, it is probably true that most Jews hope that 'death is not the end' and believe in some form of after life.

Mourner's Kaddish

And now, I pray thee, let the power of the Lord be great, according as thou hast spoken. Remember, O Lord, thy tender mercies and thy loving kindnesses; for they have been ever of old.

Mourner Magnified and sanctified be his great name in the world which he hath created according to his will. May he establish his kingdom during your life and during your days, and during the life of all the house of Israel, even speedily and at a near time, and say ye, Amen.

Cong. and Mourner Let his great name be blessed for ever and to all eternity.

Mourner Blessed, praised and glorified, exalted, extolled and honoured, magnified and lauded be the name of the Holy One, blessed be he; though he be high above all the blessings and hymns, praises and consolations, which are uttered in the world; and say ye, Amen.

Cong. Let the name of the Lord be blessed from this time forth and for evermore.

Mourner May there be abundant peace from heaven, and life for us and for all Israel; and say ye, Amen.

Cong. My help is from the Lord, who made heaven and earth.

Mourner He who maketh peace in his high places, may he make peace for us and for all Israel; and say ye, Amen.

6

The Synagogue

In good times and bad, the synagogue was able to lighten man's load, to bring him close to God, to make him feel, in Jacob's words, that 'this is none other than the House of God' (Gen. 28.17).

The synagogue has a vital role in sustaining Jewish life.

Inside a synagogue

The design and structure of the synagogue have changed over the years according to communal requirements and architectural tastes. Certain basic features have remained the same.

The building has always faced towards Jerusalem.

The holy ark is built into the wall which faces Jerusalem and in the Western hemisphere this is the eastern or *mizrach* wall.

The entire synagogue is a place of holiness, but the greatest sanctity belongs to the ark, *aron hakodesh* and its contents.

The ark dates back to the wanderings of the children of Israel in the wilderness. The Ark of the Covenant, *aron habrit*, was used to house the stone tablets of the Commandments, which Moses received at Mount Sinai. In the Temple, the ark stood in the Holy of Holies. In the synagogue, the ark became the receptacle for the Torah scrolls, which have a special sanctity of their own.

In Sephardi synagogues, this part of the building is called the *heichalor* sanctuary. In Ashkenazi synagogues an ornamental curtain conceals the doors of the ark, whereas in Sephardi synagogues the curtain is inside the ark, behind the doors. The curtain derives its name, *parochet*, from the curtain which hung in front of the Holy of Holies in the Temple.

The Eternal Light or *ner tamid* is suspended in front of the ark. It is a symbolic reminder of the continually burning menora of the Temple. The Eternal Light renews the Jew's awareness of God's shechina, or presence. It encourages respect and reverence in the sanctuary. In the wilderness Israelites were told to bring pure olive oil for the light and to ensure that the lamp was always burning. Candles were later used and now electricity.

The bima or elevated platform is traditionally placed in the centre of the building. One tradition says that since, according to ancient Jewish belief, the Temple stood at the centre of the universe so as to spread its spiritual light to all four corners of the world, so the bima, where the Torah is read, stands centrally to enable its message to be conveyed throughout the world – and, on a smaller scale, equally clearly to every corner of the synagogue. Although the congregation stands, as a sign of respect whenever the Torah scroll is removed from the ark, the congregation is allowed to sit for the reading of the Torah, because it is read from the elevated bima, which is higher than the congregation.

The first mention of the bima is as old as the fifth century BCE, in the time of Nehemiah. The Talmud speaks of it being used for communal announcements.

There are many different designs for a bima.

Besides the ark there is the rabbi's seat and there may be a pulpit.

In Orthodox synagogues, men and women sit apart. The women usually sit in a gallery or in a screened area at the back of the synagogue. The purpose is to avoid distraction. Men and women sit together in Progressive synagogues.

The decoration in some synagogues is elaborate but there are no depictions of people or animals, because of the ban on graven images (Deut. 5.8).

Synagogue appurtenances are often presented by members of the congregation in memory of a parent or other relative.

19. The ark in the Old Synagogue at Cracow, Poland

The origins of the synagogue

The origins of the synagogue are uncertain. It has always been a place of prayer and study. During the monarchy worship centred on the Temple in Jerusalem, which was built by King Solomon. There, morning and afternoon, with additional services on sabbaths and festivals, the priests would offer the prescribed sacrifices, while the Levites chanted psalms and the people watched the spectacle in silent awe.

The destruction of the Temple and the exile to Babylon in the sixth century BCE was a shattering blow to the Jewish people. It may be that the synagogue derives from this time in exile. The synagogue may have helped to sustain Jews in their faith far from their homeland and without the Temple (Ps. 137).

The earliest archaeological evidence of a synagogue dates to the third century BCE. During the Second Temple period, synagogues were common both in the Holy Land itself and in the Diaspora.

The destruction of the Second Temple by the Romans in 70 CE, also remembered on the 9th of Av, was another shattering blow. It made the synagogue even more important as a way of maintaining the Jewish faith, especially for those Jews who did not live in the land of Israel. The synagogue became, as it were, a portable homeland. The literature of the first century CE refers to numerous synagogues not only in Palestine, but also in Rome, Greece, Egypt and Babylonia. In subsequent centuries Jews have set up synagogues wherever they have settled, unless prevented by the ruling authorities. Their external architecture has varied enormously, although internally synagogues will have the features already mentioned.

Synagogue worship differed from the worship of the Temple in important ways. First, there were no sacrifices, only prayers and reading of scripture. Secondly, no priests were necessary, only someone learned enough to lead the service. Thirdly, the people took part and were not just spectators. Fourthly, synagogues could be built wherever there

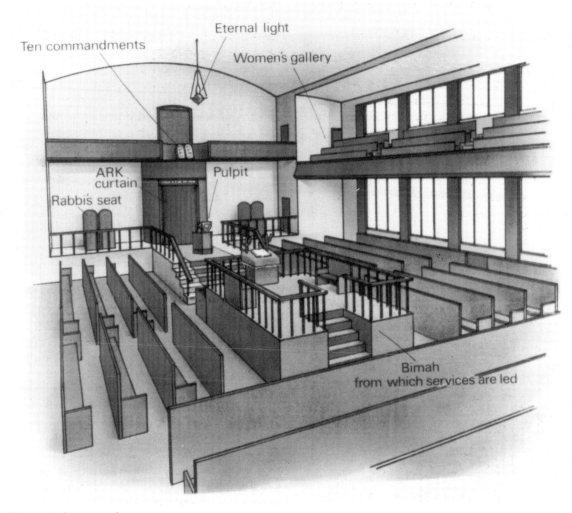

Ten commandments

Eternal light

Women's gallery

ARK
curtain

Pulpit

Rabbi's seat

Bimah
from which services are led

20. The main features of a synagogue

was a Jewish congregation. Finally, as synagogue worship emphasized language rather than ritual, it encouraged the development of a more elaborate liturgy.

With the destruction of the Temple, sacrificial offering came to an end. In Orthodox worship prayers for the rebuilding of the Temple are still said, but except for a few ultra Orthodox Jews, most Jews today do not regard this as a realistic expectation.

Schul

The synagogue, or *bet ha-keneset*, is not only a place of worship, but also of study, as the common name schul makes plain. In many synagogues, there is now a special room, *bet ha-midrash*, for study. It is a centre of communal activity as well. There are likely to be classes for children and groups for young people and for women. There will be groups to support Israel or to help Jews who are victims of persecution. Indeed there are some suggestions that the community function may overshadow the religious purpose of the synagogue.

Synagogue worship

In an Orthodox synagogue, any male member of the congregation may be invited to lead the prayers. He is called a *sheliach tzibbur*. In many synagogues the worship will be led by the rabbi or by a cantor or *chazzan*. In Progressive synagogues, women may also perform these roles.

Jews are encouraged to join together in the synagogue for daily prayers, although these prayers may be said at home. There are three times of prayer, with additional services on sabbaths and festivals. Ten men are required to make a minyan for prayer.

The morning service

At the morning service it is usual to wear a tallit or prayer shawl and to put on tefillin (see ch. 4). Words of meditation are said as these are put on as a reminder of the spiritual meaning of the physical actions.

The prayer, tefillah, is preceded by the recitation of the Shema.

The morning prayer consists of eight parts:

The morning blessings, *birkot ha-shahar* in twenty-two sections;

The biblical and Talmudic passages, which speak about the sacrifices of the Temple;

Liturgical hymns and psalms;

The Shema;

The *Tefillah/'Amidah* or Eighteen Benedictions;

Intercession;

Readings from the Torah on Sabbaths and Festivals and on Mondays and Thursdays;

The end of morning prayer.

This may be shortened and simplified on weekdays and perhaps elaborated on Sabbaths, when there may be a sermon. Instrumental music is not allowed in Orthodox synagogues, but is permitted in Progressive ones.

The morning service is printed in Jewish prayer books, as are other daily services, the services for the Sabbath, for festivals and for rites of passage.

The rabbi

Although the rabbi may lead prayer, the title means 'My Master'. This title was applied to Palestinian sages whose major task in Talmudic times was that of a teacher. The rabbi was someone who was an expert in Torah and could decide cases of Jewish law. At that time, he usually earned his living by other work.

Today most rabbis are paid by their congregation – or technically, are compensated for what they would have earned if they were not occupied in rabbinical duties. A rabbi of a large congregation might receive a salary similar to that of a teacher. He would often have to buy his own house.

A congregational rabbi today serves his congregation as a teacher, preacher, expert on religious law, officiant at marriages and funerals and as a pastoral counsellor. He does not have priestly functions.

After a period of training at a rabbinic college or perhaps at a yeshivah, which is a traditional centre for the study of talmudic and rabbinic texts, a person will receive ordination as a rabbi from an already ordained rabbi. In Progressive Judaism, women may be rabbis. Not all rabbis will serve congregations. Some may be chaplains, some will specialize in rules about kosher food, others may be in a teaching position and others may have an administrative role in a Jewish organization.

Prayer and Study

Prayer

Prayer without words is possible, but the tendency to verbalize is strong. Prayers include praise, confession and supplication. Supplication suggests that God can be influenced by prayer. The Talmud has stories of men of exceptional piety who were able to bring a drought to an end by their prayers. The synagogue liturgy includes prayers for recovery from illness. On the whole Judaism stresses the effect on the person praying. The influential teacher Rabban Gamaliel III said, 'Make God's will your will, so that He may make your will His will.' A characteristic of the prayers of the synagogue are their emphasis on blessing God.

Judaism teaches that every human being has been given free will. He may incline himself to the good or bad. When a person does wrong he may confess and seek God's forgiveness. If he has offended another person, he must seek reconciliation with that person.

For the Orthodox Jew especially, the set prayers are an obligation – they are to be offered to God in sincerity, but the spirituality of the person praying is secondary to the fulfillment of the duty.

21. The Old Synagogue Maran Beit Joseph, Safad, Israel

Mystical Judaism

Jews who belonged to the mystical Chasidic movement, which dates back to the eighteenth century, reacted strongly against the tendency to see prayer as an obligation to be discharged almost mechanically at fixed times. They encouraged the worshipper to put his whole body and soul into prayer. They stressed music and dancing and they borrowed tunes freely from external sources. They also disregarded the canonical hours of prayer. As one teacher put it, 'People have souls, not clocks.' For them the purpose of prayer is to seek an often ecstatic union with God.

The mystical tradition is rooted in the search for personal communion with the Divine – evident in the Bible. A number of rabbis were also mystics. The mysticism of this period centred on two points:

1. Speculation about the generation of the universe in the account of creation and about the relationship between God and his world;

2. Contemplative mysticism surrounding the vision of the divine chariot, or throne, based on the description in the Book of Ezekiel.

Teaching on the second subject was only for the mature student. There were many warnings about the danger of mysticism.

In the Middle Ages, Safad in northern Palestine became a centre for mystical teaching, where key figures, such as Rabbi Moses Cordovero and Rabbi Isaac Luria (1534–72) settled. The latter taught a mystical messianism which captured the imagination of his followers and reached a wide audience through his books. This mystical literature became known as the kabbalah.

The mystical influence spread to Eastern Europe, where it was given new direction by Israel Baal Shem Tov (1700–60), often called the Besht. A number of Chasidic masters gathered around him. Together they stressed the everyday relevance of mysticism. When in this century Jews fled from Eastern Europe to the USA, many Chasidic Jews established themselves there, especially in Brooklyn. From there, a number have made their way to Israel.

Two continuing characteristics of Jewish mysticism are the sense of the unknowability of God – our images are only approximations – and the personal longing for intimacy with the divine. Both are expressed in 'The Hymn of Glory', a mediaeval composition which still has an honoured place in the Ashkenazi liturgy.

The Hymn of Glory

Songs I weave and tunes I utter, for my soul doth pant
    for thee.
Longing in thy powerful shade to know thy secret
    mystery.
As thy glory I describe, my mind desires to soar above,
So I sing about thy glory, glorifying thy name with
    love.

All unseeing I sing thy glory, all unknowing I speak of
    thee
By thy faithful prophets showing images of mystery.
Calling on thy works they named thee, picturing thy
    power and might;
Drawing on thy deeds they framed thee, who wert
    hidden from their sight.
Every vision paints its picture, but in essence thou art
    One,
Full of years or youthful victor, flushed with pride of
    battles won.

Study

The importance of Talmud Torah, religious education, is stressed in both the Bible and rabbinic texts. Already in Pharisaic times there was the start of a network of schools for the religious instruction of all. The poor and orphans were educated at the community's expense. The primary responsibility for children's education, however, rests with their parents. A Jew is expected to know enough Hebrew to follow the synagogue services and to read the scripture, but this is not always the case. Study should continue throughout life. It includes reading and discussing both biblical and rabbinic texts.

The love for God which prayer and study promote should show itself in an ethical life. Love for God is shown by love of one's neighbour (Lev. 19.18). Putting Judaism into practice includes being honest in business dealings, treating others with respect, keeping one's temper under control, avoiding malicious gossip, assisting those with a burden, returning lost property, caring for the handicapped, visiting the sick, responding to others in a warm spirit and generally regarding the rights and feelings of others as being as important as one's own, as well as giving to charity.

7

Torah and Jewish Literature

'Happy are you, O Israel, whom God has chosen to make the Torah your heritage.'

These words are said three times during the liturgy on *Simchat Torah,* the festival of 'Rejoicing in the Law', which comes at the end of *Sukkot.*

The word 'law' can conjure up different pictures in our mind: perhaps of slowing down on a motorway, because we see a police car ahead of us; perhaps we have a picture of a stern judge giving sentence. A look at the picture of Jews rejoicing in the Law or a reading of Ps. 119.89–112 gives a different impression. Here the law is seen as a privilege and delight. It was given by God to the chosen people at Mount Sinai after they had been rescued from slavery in Egypt.

What does Torah mean?

So far we have usually translated Torah by the word 'law', but 'law' is too narrow in meaning. 'Way of life' might be better.

The translation 'law' has arisen partly through Greek influence, because when the Hebrew scriptures were translated into Greek in the third century BCE – in what is known as the Septuagint (see under Chanukah in ch. 3) – the word Torah was translated by the Greek word *nomos,* law. Torah includes matters of personal morality as well as matters of criminal or civil law. In includes directions for the cult and purification. There are instructions about what to eat or not to eat. The purpose was to show the people of Israel how to live as 'the

people of God', i.e., how to live as a healthy and contented community, as 'a light to the Gentiles'. Judaism does not have a doctrine of original sin. Like Islam, it assumes that people are able to understand and to obey God's will, even if they fail and often need forgiveness.

The word Torah is used in several ways:

1. Torah originally referred to an individual teaching communicated to the people by a spokesperson of God, such as a prophet or priest.

2. Torah is often a name given to the first five books of the Bible, which are known as the books of Moses. These books have primary importance and Jews read the rest of the Bible in their light.

3. Sometimes Torah is used to mean the whole Hebrew Bible, which Jews often call Tenakh or Tanach. This is an abbreviation of the initial letter of the Hebrew words for the three main parts of the Bible: Torah (Teaching), Nevi'im (Prophets) and Ketuvim (Writings).

4. Torah came to be used collectively for the entire corpus of the teaching which, it was believed, God had revealed through Moses to the Israelites at Mount Sinai. This includes the written Torah (the books of the Bible) and the oral Torah, or traditional teaching and interpretation, preserved by the rabbis and which is believed also to have been given to Moses on Mount Sinai.

5. Torah can even be used to mean the whole corpus of Jewish religious literature and teaching. There is an old saying that 'Even the everyday

22. The scroll of the Torah carried in procession

conversation of the learned is Torah and needs to be studied.'

Orthodox Judaism recognizes the authority of both the written and oral Torah.

> Moses received Torah from Sinai and passed it on to Joshua, and Joshua to the Elders, and the Elders to the Prophets; and the Prophets passed it on to the men of the Great Assembly. They said three things: Be careful in giving judgment, raise up many disciples, and make a fence around the Torah.
>
> Rabbinic saying

Although Christians and Jews share many of the same scriptures, they approach them with different presuppositions. Christians tend to regard the Psalms and the Prophets as the most important parts of the 'Old Testament' and are mostly likely to hear these read in church. For Jews the first five books of the Bible are the most important.

The term 'Old Testament' may suggest that these scriptures have been outdated or superseded by the Christian scriptures. To avoid this some Jews and Christians today prefer the phrase 'Hebrew Bible', because almost all of the Tenach is written in Hebrew. To Jews, of course, the first part of the Bible is simply the Bible.

The tendency to read the 'Old Testament' as foreshadowing the events of the New Testament, which is called the 'typological' method of interpreting the 'Old Testament' has, in recent years, been questioned by many Christians, because it fails both to interpret scripture in its historical context and to recognize that the whole Bible is the Word of God.

Revelation

Is the Bible to be taken as literally the word of God?

In Judaism there is argument about the nature of revelation and the extent to which scripture should be seen as a human creation as well as divine self-disclosure. This is a major point of disagreement between Orthodox Jews on the one hand and Progressive Jews on the other. The latter will also be more ready to question the oral tradition.

The traditional belief is that the whole of the Pentateuch was revealed to Moses. The Bible does itself refer to Moses writing some things down. Few critical scholars, however, accept the Mosaic authorship of the Pentateuch, although this was virtually unquestioned by both Jews and Christians until the last century.

Orthodox Jews insist that the five books of Moses were revealed by God. Some picture God dictating the words to Moses, but other Orthodox scholars take a more nuanced position. Rabbi Dr Norman Solomon has written: 'Our attitude towards sacred texts, in particular the Bible and the Talmud, has changed under the impact of modern scholarship. We have learned to see them as the record of the Israelite and Jewish response to God over a period of some thousands of years, and in varying cultural environments. We therefore try to relate statements to their social-historical contexts, and we recognize the views which then emerge as attempts, not always perfectly executed and by no means always mutually consistent, to grapple with major issues. Bible and Talmud are not "proof texts" but guides to life, aids to our rediscovery and reformulation of the teachings and insights they enshrine' (*Judaism and World Religion*, Macmillan 1991, p. 7).

Progressive Jews acknowledge the human element in scripture. The Reform rabbi Dr Jonathan Romain writes: 'Torah contains the word of God, although interpreted and written down by human beings' (*Faith and Practice*, p. 244). The 'Columbus Platform', a statement drawn up by Reform Jews in Columbus, Ohio, in 1937, says: 'Revelation is a continuous process, confined to no one group and to no one age. Yet the people of Israel, through its prophets and sages, achieved unique insight in the realm of religious truth. The Torah, both written and oral, enshrines Israel's ever-growing consciousness of God and of the moral law. It preserves the historical precedents, sanctions and norms of Jewish life, and seeks to mould it in the patterns of goodness and holiness. Being products of historical processes, certain of its laws have lost their binding force with the passing of the conditions which called them forth. But as a depository of permanent spiritual ideals, the Torah remains the dynamic source of the life of Israel. Each age has the obligation to adapt the teachings of the Torah to its basic needs in consonance with the genius of Judaism.'

The different emphases on revelation and tradition are shown in the way Torah's commands (*mitzvot*) are interpreted.

23. A rabbi shows a scroll to visiting school children

Respect for scripture

The great importance of Torah for Jews of all traditions is shown in high respect for the scriptures. The scriptures are written on scrolls. The care taken in their preparation and preservation indicates the sacredness of scripture for the Jewish people.

The material used is parchment. This must be from an animal of which the flesh is allowed for human consumption which means it is kosher. The writing calls for extreme care. There must be no mistake, so the *sofer* or scribe constantly rereads his work and it is checked by others. The writing of the text is in columns, beginning at the right upper edge of a column. Each column consists of perhaps forty lines of equal length. Words should not be broken up, so the *sofer* carefully spaces the words.

Square writing has been used for two thousand years. Classical Hebrew writing consists only of consonants, so the reader needs to know what vowels to use. The ink is a deep permanent black and the *sofer* uses a quill from a ritually clean bird – often a goose. A scroll may be repaired, but when it is past repair, it is put in a jar and buried or stored in a special room called a *genizah*.

The scrolls, which may have ornate casings or dressings, are kept in what is usually called the 'holy ark', in front of which is a decorative curtain. A central feature of a morning Sabbath service is the opening of the ark and the removal and carrying of a scroll in procession, for which everyone stands, to the *bimah* or reading desk. In the synagogue service members of the congregation are called forward to read part of the readings for the week, from the Torah and then from the Prophets.

How is Torah interpreted in daily life?

Revelation may be unchanging, but life changes. How is an unchanging revelation applied to daily life? Revelation, however authoritative, needs interpretation.

In a Jerusalem hotel, one of the lifts may be marked 'Sabbath Lift'. This is the one which goes up and down automatically on the Sabbath stopping at every floor. This means that passengers avoid on the Sabbath the work of pressing a button to call a lift.

The task of interpreting the Torah to daily life is the work of the rabbis. In doing this, they refer back to an enormous amount of literature which sums up the teaching of previous rabbis. Progressive Jews may be prepared to question this tradition whilst Orthodox rabbis are not.

Some Orthodox rabbis, as we have seen, claim that the Oral tradition itself goes back to Moses. Historical study suggests that it was during the Exile in Babylon (586–538 BCE) that the organized interpretation of scripture and the formulation of the oral Law began. Indeed adapting to life in Exile must have called for considerable efforts to apply the law in new circumstances. The traditional view is that this activity was initiated by Ezra and carried on by the 'men of the Great Assembly' and thereafter by the *soferim* or scribes and by the Pharisees.

Two principles were applied in interpreting Torah:

1. One was, metaphorically, to build a fence around the law.

An example comes from the kosher or dietary regulations.

One Gentile went to a kosher restaurant and had ordered chicken. He asked the waiter to bring him some butter instead of the margarine provided. The waiter refused. Why?

There is a biblical law (Ex. 23.19 and 34.26; Deut. 14.21) which forbids the boiling of a kid in its mother's milk – perhaps as a protest against a pagan fertility rite. The rabbis to ensure that this did not happen 'put a fence around the law' and prohibited the mixing of meat with milk or milk products. If you have meat at a meal, you do not have dairy products. Indeed in many Israeli cafeterias there are two counters – one for meat dishes and one for dairy products. (See further on kosher in ch. 4.)

2. The second principle was to make explicit what was implicit or unsaid.

24. An eighteenth century Torah crown from Poland

For example the original injunction 'an eye for an eye' was meant to limit the vengeance that a person might seek – i.e. 'no more than an eye for an eye'. Yet two thousand years ago, the rabbis decided that what God really meant was 'the value of an eye for an eye'. Financial compensation was therefore substituted for physical disfigurement.

One needs to be very careful to see how believers use their sacred texts and not take words out of context.

Another example is the interpretation of 'You shall not curse the deaf.' This was taken to mean you should not curse anyone, *not even* the deaf, who cannot hear that you are cursing them.

The rabbinic literature

Rabbis today look back to Pharisees as their spiritual forefathers and their interpretations of Torah reflect the teaching of the Pharisees and of subsequent rabbis. There are several collections of their teachings which are still used today.

After the Fall of Jerusalem in 70 CE, the Pharisaic teachings were collected, classified and expanded by the rabbis. Led by Rabbi Johanan ben Zakkai they settled at Jamnia, near the Judaean coast. There the supreme assembly (Sanhedrin) summarized the legal teachings of Hillel and other rabbis. They fixed the canon of scripture, organized the daily prayers, and transferred some of the Temple observances to the synagogue.

The following centuries were a very creative period in the interpretation of the scriptures, known as Midrash, and the topic-by-topic exposition of Jewish Law, known as Mishnah.

The Mishnah, the collection of legal expositions, itself became the basis for study and the further discussions are collected in the Talmud (a word which means both 'learning' and 'teaching'). The Talmud is organized around the Mishnah, which it reproduces instalment by instalment in full. After each instalment there is the Gemara, which examines the Mishnah text in great detail.

There are two versions of the Talmud: Yerushalmi and Bavli. The Palestinian or, rather misleadingly called Jerusalem Talmud, the Yerushalmi, was completed about 400 CE. The other, the Babylonian Talmud, or Bavli, or Babli, was completed sometime after 500 CE. Neither cover all the tractates of the Mishnah. The Babylonian Talmud, usually regarded as the more authoritative, only covers 36 tractates, but even so it occupies 15,000 pages in the English translation, published by the Soncino Press.

The Midrash, the collection of interpretations of scripture, and the Talmud, which is a literature rather than just a book, became the basis for the legal, or halachic, discussions of rabbinic Judaism. Study of rabbinic material is a lifetime's work.

Example of Midrash

Deut. 15.11 'Thou shalt open wide your hand to your brother' is explained as meaning you should give according to particular needs. To him for whom bread is suitable give bread: . . . to him for whom it is fitting to put food in his mouth, put it.

Great attention is paid to detail and the exact wording of the text. For example, Rabbi Meir found scriptural warrant for belief in the resurrection in the verse Ex. 15.1, 'Then will Moses and then will the children of Israel sing this song unto the Lord.' The text says 'will sing' not 'sang', which implies the future and therefore the resurrection (Cf. Mark 12.18–27).

Example of Mishnah

These are the differences between the House of Shammai and the House of Hillel with regard to the meal.

The House of Shammai says, 'One recites the blessing over the day first, and then the blessing over the wine.' The House of Hillel says, 'One recites the blessing over the wine first, and then the blessing over the day.'

The House of Shammai says, 'They wash the hands first, and then mix the cup.' The House of Hillel says, 'They mix the cup first, and then wash the hands.'

(It is interesting that differences of teaching are preserved in the tradition.)

The first authoritative compilation of rabbinic teaching was made by Rabbi Judah ha-Nasi. This was committed to writing soon after 200 CE. We know a little about Judah ha-Nasi and this helps to make the documents more alive. The *nasi* of the Sandedrin was the recognized patriarch of the Jews and was given the right to collect taxes for Jewish institutions, to appoint judges for Jewish courts and to send official emissaries to the Diaspora communities. Judah ha-Nasi (170–217) was highly venerated and known just as 'Rabbi'. He was a wealthy and cultivated man, who spoke both Hebrew and Greek and who kept on good terms with the Romans.

Not all the oral traditions known to the early rabbis were included in the Mishnah. Rabbi Judah only included those he endorsed or thought worthy of mention. A supplement was therefore collected known as Tosefta, which is considerably larger.

The distinction between Midrash and Mishnah is the most important way of classifying rabbinic literature, but there are other ways of which it may be useful to be aware. One is by subject matter. Halakhah, from the Hebrew for 'to walk', deals with behaviour – covering a larger area of life than just what we regard as legal matters. Haggadah means 'narration'. It includes everything that is not about behaviour and includes theology, history, legend and parable. In the Haggadah, for example, idolatry is condemned even more severely than in the Bible. A Midrash or commentary on Numbers declares that 'He who commits idolatry denies the Ten Commandments, and all that was commanded to Moses, to the Prophets and to the Patriarchs . . . He who renounces idolatry is as if he professed the whole Law.'

Rabbinic literature can also be classified according to its date. The major distinction is between material from the period 70–200 CE, which is known as the Age of the Tannaim and which is recorded in the Mishnah and material from the period 200–500 CE, which is known as the Age of the Amoraim and which is recorded in the Talmud. Tannaitic literature is generally Palestinian and written in Hebrew. Amoraic literature may be Palestinian or Babylonian, and is characteristically written in Aramaic. Some of the tannaitic material is said to come from the school of Rabbi Akiva and his disciple Rabbi Simeon.

Later writings

Translations, texts and commentaries

Scripture may need to be translated into a language more familiar to the hearer or listener. But translation is also interpretation or it may be *mis*interpretation. To guard against this it became customary in ancient Palestinian synagogues to employ a competent interpreter, known as a meturgeman, who translated the scriptures orally – a verse at a time, in the case of Torah, or three verses at a time, in the case of the Prophets. The practice was superseded by the publication of an approved Aramaic translation of the Pentateuch, called the Targum Onkelos. Targum is Hebrew for translation and Onkelos the name of its reputed author. Dating from the second century CE, this Targum gained an authority next only to the Hebrew text and can indicate how verses were understood at that time.

Not content with the Talmud, Jews have continued to write a great variety of literature. The Bible needed to be copied. Great care was taken with its transmission and a strict discipline, known as the masorah, was developed. Even so there were mistakes and differences, so Jewish scholars at Tiberias in Palestine from the seventh century gradually established an authoritative text. The work was effectively completed by Aaron ben Asher in the tenth century. The result became known as the Masoretic Text. Translations into new languages became necessary and also commentaries. The most famous commentary is by Rashi, who lived in Northern France. There are also commentaries on rabbinic literature of which the best known is by Maimonides.

Maimonides

Moses Maimonides was the foremost intellectual figure of mediaeval Judaism. He made a lasting contribution as a jurist, philosopher and scientist. His works, translated into Latin, influenced Spinoza and Leibniz, two great European philosophers. He was born in Cordova in Spain in 1135. Before he was thirteen, Cordova was captured by the Almohads, a fanatical Muslim sect. Eventually the family fled to Fez, in Morocco, where he added the study of medicine to his interest in rabbinics and Greek philosophy. After a few years, a close companion was arrested for practising Judaism, so Maimonides fled, first to Palestine and then to Cairo. Safe now from persecution – as Egypt allowed considerable freedom to Jews – Maimonides now faced family problems. His father died and his brother, a prosperous jewelry merchant on whom Moses relied for support, died in a shipwreck, taking the family fortune with him. Moses had to support the family and took up practising medicine. He became so well known that he became court physician to the Sultan Saladin.

He continued his writings about Judaism. Besides his *Mishneh Torah*, he wrote the well-known *Guide for the Perplexed* in which he called for a more rational philosophy of Judaism. This work was a major contribution to the accommodation between science, philosophy and religion. It was written in Arabic, but soon translated into Hebrew and Latin. His advanced views, of course, provoked some opposition.

Maimonides often complained that the pressures of his many duties robbed him of peace and undermined his health. He died in 1204 and was buried in Tiberias. It is worth noting the extent to which people travelled in the mediaeval Mediterranean world and we should be aware, too, of the brilliance of Jewish and Muslim scholarship at a time when Christendom was far less advanced.

Maimonides' Thirteen Fundamental Principles of the Jewish Faith is a well known summary of Jewish belief.

Responsa

Another category of post-talmudic literature are the Responsa or Questions and Answers given by famous scholars on questions of Law and practice. The collections of Responsa run to thousands of volumes and cover a wide range of subjects. Also, after the completion of the Talmud, the need was felt for a systematic presentation of Jewish Law, distilling the definitive legislation and bringing it up to date. The greatest recapitulation of the Law was the *Mishneh Torah*, or Recapitulation of the Law, popularly known as 'The Mighty Hand', *Yad ha-Chazakah*, by Maimonides (1134–1204). The Ashkenazi Jews also produced codes. Subsequently there were commentaries on the codes.

Prayer books

Amongst other writings, Maimonides produced what was in effect a prayer book or seder, which was to have a lasting influence on Sephardi liturgy. Ashkenazi liturgy was influenced by the prayer books of Rashi and Simchah ben Samuel Vitry. Until that time liturgy had been mainly transmitted orally. Since the invention of printing, numerous prayer books have been printed, often with translations into the local language. The best known English version, used by the United (Orthodox) Synagogues in Britain and some other countries, is known as the Singer Prayer Book, as it was translated by Revd Simeon Singer. It has Hebrew on one page and English on the facing page. This book is used by some Orthodox congregations in North America. Other congregations use the translation by either A. Hyman Charlap or by Philip Birnbaum. In both North America and Britain, the Art Scroll Siddur is, however, quickly growing in popularity and replacing older versions of the prayer book. The divisions in Judaism have produced a variety of prayer books, and those of the Reform Synagogue in Britain, edited by Rabbi Jonathan Magonet and Rabbi Lionel Blue, are especially impressive.

Zohar

Jewish mysticism has its roots in antiquity, but much of the literature dates from the Middle Ages, when it became known as *kabbalah*, or 'received tradition'. It is theosophical speculation on the ultimate mysteries, especially the creation story and Ezekiel's vision of the heavenly chariot. Its mediaeval development was first in Provence about 1200 CE and then in Spain. There towards the end of the thirteenth century, the *Sefar ha-Zohar*, or *Book of Splendour* was produced. The Zohar became an authoritative text and the basis of subsequent mystical thought, especially of Isaac Luria (1534–72). *Kabbalah* also profoundly influenced Chasidism, as we saw in the previous chapter.

Other literature

There is a wealth of other Jewish literature, which grows out of Torah. This includes books of moral guidance and devotion. Influential too have been books of philosophy. Perhaps the greatest Jewish philosopher was Baruch Spinoza (1632–77), although he belongs more to European philosophy, despite strong Jewish influence. Moses Mendelssohn (1729–86), a child of the Enlightenment, wrote in the spirit of eighteenth-century Rationalism. He sought to encourage integration between Jewish and European culture, which had the unintended effect also of encouraging assimilation.

In this century, perhaps the two most influential Jewish philosophers have been Franz Rosenzweig (1886–1929), known especially for *Star of Redemption* and Martin Buber (1878–1965), remembered especially for *I and Thou*.

Jewish poetry deserves a mention, as does Jewish humour and fiction. Probably the greatest Hebrew poet was from Spain: Judah Halevi. Much Jewish fiction is in Yiddish. Maybe the most famous contemporary writer is Elie Wiesel, who was born in 1928 and is a survivor of the Nazi concentration camps. Much of his writing reflects on the horror of the Holocaust.

There has also been a flowering of Hebrew literature in Israel.

Jewish writing – in many languages – is a continuing activity. The creative contribution of Jews to other forms of the media and arts and to all aspects of intellectual life in many countries is remarkable. It is a reminder that Jews still have a vital part to play in human culture.

8

From 1800 BCE to 1800 CE

I will sing of the Lord's great love for ever; with my mouth I will make your faithfulness known through all generations (Ps. 89.1).

History as it is retold from generation to generation within a faith community, for example at festivals, and its reconstruction by critical scholars can be very different. The Bible says that it is the Lord who called Israel into being and who has sustained his people through the centuries. The story of Abraham begins with the words, 'The Lord said to Abram' (Gen. 12.1). At every Passover, Jews remember that it was the Lord who rescued them 'with a mighty hand' from Pharaoh, king of Egypt. Second Isaiah speaks of the Persian ruler Cyrus, who allowed the Jews to return from exile in Babylon as 'the Lord's annointed' (Isa. 45.1). There are even some Jews today who see the rebirth of the State of Israel as God's miraculous answer to the horror of the Holocaust. The historian, however, does not explain events by reference to divine action.

Beginnings

Abraham, it has been said, was the founder of the Jewish people, Moses the founder of the Jewish religion – but that is an over-simplification. The biblical story, of course, begins with God's creation of the world. This is traditionally dated to 5753 BCE, each New Year beginning at Rosh Hashanah in September or October. There are those Jews who accept the story of creation in its literal sense, whilst others see it as a myth, perhaps an adaptation of a still older Mesopotamian myth. That the history of the Jews begins with the creation sets their particular history in the context of the history of all humankind. All people are descended from common ancestors. This is significant when considering the idea of a 'chosen' people. It is also important for the development of monotheism that the Israelites believed that their God was the creator of the world and Lord of History and that as history had a beginning it also has a goal.

Already the words 'Jews' and 'Israelites' have been used. 'Hebrews' also is often used of the earliest ancestors – or the patriarchs – Abraham, Isaac and Jacob. Jacob, after he had wrestled with God, was given the name Israel (Gen. 32.28). His descendants were called 'children of Israel' or 'Israelites'. The tribe that claimed descent from Jacob's fourth son was called Judah. When the two kingdoms split, the northern was known as Israel and the southern as Judah. When the Israelites returned from exile in Babylon, the puppet state which centred on Jerusalem was again called Judah. From this, via the Greek, we get the words Jew and Judaism. Judaism is a relatively new word, which originally was used to mean 'Jewish identity' rather than a system of beliefs. Some people tend to use 'Judaism' of the religion and way of life based on the Law that was developed by Ezra, the Pharisees and the rabbis in contrast to the religion of ancient Israel. Others speak of different periods of Judaism.

Abraham

Abraham is regarded as the father of the Jewish people and indeed as the father of many peoples. Christians and Muslims also look back to their common father Abraham. To Jews, as the circumcision service says, the covenant with Abraham was confirmed unto Isaac and unto Jacob.

Whilst there is no independent evidence with which to corroborate the biblical narrative, archaeological discoveries in this century provide a context in which to place Abraham. They also discourage wilder speculation that the patriarchs were mythical beings or the personifications of tribes. Indeed at Hebron, visitors are shown the cave of Machpelah where tradition claims that Abraham and Sarah were buried.

25. Abraham's tomb at Hebron

The story, however, starts in Ur, in Mesopotamia, which is near the mouth of the river Euphrates at the top of the Persian Gulf. The Mesopotamian civilization had been established by the end of the fourth millenium BCE. It was characterized by the development of agriculture, city states and then by the discovery of the wheel, of pottery and by the invention of writing. The culture probably reached its height in the middle of the third millenium, but around 1950 BCE, the Third Dynasty of Ur came to

an end and the city was sacked and destroyed. There followed a period of instability and tension.

About this time, Abraham's father Terah set out from Ur and travelled north along the Euphrates to Haran. The religion in Mesopotamia was a developed polytheism, with gods ranged in a complex pantheon. The Bible admits that the Israelites' ancestors worshipped 'other gods' in Mesopotamia. In Haran, Abraham heard the voice of God telling him to leave his country and go to the land that God would show him. Abraham journeyed into Canaan and God promised this septuagenarian that his barren wife Sarai or Sarah would have a child. Whilst waiting, Abraham had a son, Ishmael, by Sarah's maidservant Hagar. Hagar and Ishmael were expelled, but Ishmael came to be seen as the forefather of the Arab and Muslim people. Eventually Sarah gave birth to Isaac. The story of the 'sacrifice of Isaac' is presumably a rejection of child-sacrifice (although feminist theologians wonder what Sarah thought about it). Towards the end of his life, Abraham ensured that Isaac married a girl from his own people in Mesopotamia (Gen. 24).

Abraham is pictured as a righteous man, committed to God, peace-loving, but when necessary to rescue Lot, willing to take action. He pleaded with God to save Sodom. In the course of time, Jewish tradition has increasingly elevated the status of Abraham, making him the 'servant' of God, 'a friend of God', one 'whom no one equals in renown'. In later Judaism, his life is adorned with miracles and legends and virtues. Two apocryphal writings are devoted to him: one about his revelations (the Abraham Apocalypse) and the other about his journey to Paradise (the Testament of Abraham). The Bible does not hide his faults, but in tradition he becomes a model of all virtue. Rabbinic Judaism claimed that he obeyed all the laws of the written and oral Torah. To this day his name is commemorated in the liturgy, especially on New Year's Day and in the first praise of the Eighteen Benedictions.

Some women rabbis have recently attempted also to see the matriarchs as role models. Attention, for example, has been given to rabbinic references to the relationship of Rachel and Leah. Both were married to Jacob and one might have expected jealousy between them, especially as Jacob obviously preferred Rachel. One Midrash, however, says that Rachel only conceived her longed-for child when she, Leah and their two handmaids all prayed together that God would remove the curse of barrenness from Rachel.

Abraham's descendants, Joseph, his brothers and his father Jacob eventually settled in Egypt, probably when the country was ruled by the Hyskos or 'foreign chiefs', who ruled from about 1690–1580 BCE. There they became slaves, until they were rescued by Moses.

Moses

There is argument about which Pharaoh oppressed the Israelites, as the name is not given in the Bible. Some date the Exodus to 1440 BCE, when Thuthmosis III was the ruler. A date nearly two hundred years later fits the archaeological evidence better. Towards the end of the fourteenth century BCE, a religious revolution threatened to destroy the mighty Egyptian empire. The young king Amenophis IV declared that the sun god, Aten, was the sole deity, but the Aten cult was bitterly opposed by the priesthood and the masses. When Akhenaten, as Amenophis IV called himself, died or was assassinated, his heresy was destroyed, although one wonders if there were still some secret believers who influenced Moses during his education at the Egyptian court. Akhenaten's successors set out to reassert Egypt's power, making war inevitable with the powerful Hittite empire. Sethos I regained control of Palestine. His successor Ramesses II (c. 1290–1224), after a ten-year struggle against the Hittites, made peace. He then embarked on a big building programme. This was at Pithom and Raamses in north-east Egypt, not far from Goshen where the Hebrews lived. Exodus implies that it was easy for Moses to visit the court to confront Pharaoh. Probably the Hebrews were forced

to labour at building these cities. Another clue to the dating is that excavations suggest that the cities which the Hebrews claimed to have captured in Canaan were destroyed about 1250 BCE.

Some people try to find historical events to 'explain' the miracles of the Exodus. There is argument too about numbers. The Bible suggests the whole people of Israel were slaves in Egypt, whereas some modern scholars suggest only one tribe went into Egypt. The Bible talks of 600,000 men bearing arms, as well as women and children – perhaps two to three million people. Yet Exodus 1.15–22 suggests that two midwives could adequately care for the needs of the Hebrews.

The name Moses – Hebrew 'Moshe' – is derived from the Egyptian *mose*, 'is born' and is found in Egyptian names such as 'Thuthmosis' – 'The god Thuth is born'. Perhaps Moses shortened his name when he returned to his people. The Bible says little about his childhood and youth at the Egyptian court, but he seems to have received instruction in religious, civil and military matters and this was to equip him for leadership later in life. It is even suggested that the Sinai covenant may have been modelled on the form in which the Hittites made treaties with their subjects and that Moses learned about these at the Egyptian court.

Somehow, Moses became aware of his Hebrew descent, but when his murder of an Egyptian official became known, he fled to Midian. There he looked after the flocks of Jethro, whose daughter, Zipporah, he married. Possibly Jethro already worshipped the Lord (Ex. 18.8).

As he was tending the flocks, Moses had a decisive encounter with God. Approaching the burning bush, he heard God say, 'I am the God of your father, the God of Abraham, the God of Isaac, the God of Jacob.' Although he was in a strange land, the God who spoke to him was the God of his fathers, and he was calling Moses to bring the children of Israel out of slavery in Egypt into the Promised Land. Then Moses asked God his name. 'I am who I am,' was the reply, or 'I will be what I will be.'

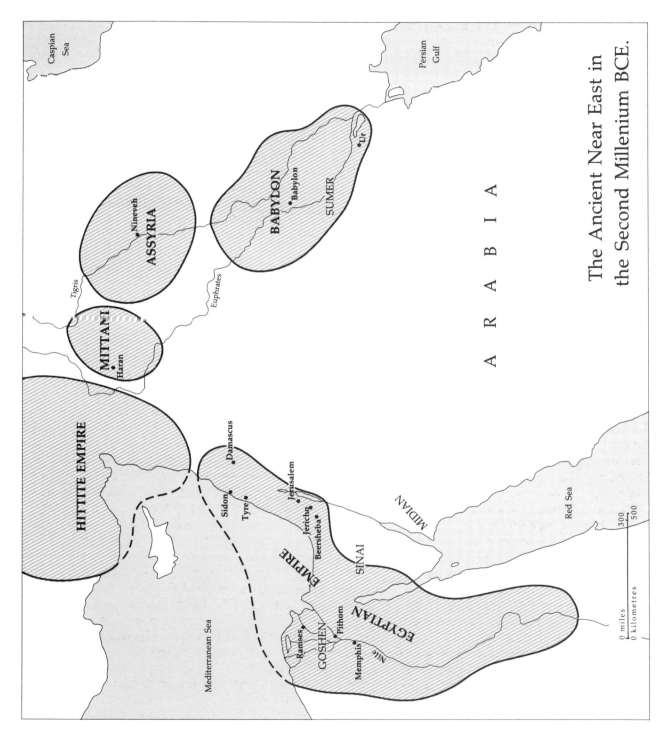

The Ancient Near East in
the Second Millenium BCE.

There has been much discussion of this verse. The word translated Lord (v.15) is equivalent to Yahweh, which is derived in Exodus 3.13–5 from the verb *hayah*, perhaps in its causative form. This God is identified with El' Elyon or El Shaddai, as the High God known to Abraham and the patriarchs. According to Exodus 6.2, Yahweh is a new name. 'God also said to Moses, "I am the Lord. I appeared to Abraham, to Isaac and to Jacob as God Almighty (El Shaddai), but by my name of Lord, I did not make myself known".'

The word for God in Genesis 12.1 is in fact Yahweh, but that is probably the editor's choice. Some scholars distinguish various sources in the first books of the Bible. According to the 'Yahwistic' source or J, Yahweh had been known and worshipped since the time of Adam: but according to the 'Priestly' source, P, the name of Yahweh was first revealed to Moses. In Canaan, the patriarchs, who at Haran had worshipped 'other gods', came in contact with El and adopted him. They spoke of God as El, or El Elyon (God Most High) or El Shaddai (God, the One of the Mountains). He was the God of Abraham's tribe, but this was monolatry – worship of one God – rather than monotheism, the belief that there is only one God. For Moses God is Lord of history, as it is he who will rescue the Israelites from Egypt and he is Lord of nature.

26. The Mount Sinai range

The story of Israel's escape from Egypt has already been recalled when we looked at Passover. The Israelites' journeyings brought them to Mount Sinai, the 'mountain of God'. Although the location is disputed, there seems no decisive reason to reject the traditional identification of Mount Sinai (Horeb) with Jabal Musa, in the granite range at the southern tip of the Sinai Peninsula. It was there at Sinai that God made a covenant with his people. From Sinai Moses led the Israelites towards the Promised Land of Canaan, although he did not enter it himself.

There have, of course, been numerous estimates of Moses and they depend in part on how reliable one considers the biblical narrative to be. In Judaism, he is a central figure. In the Bible he is spoken of as a prophet and in rabbinical Judaism he is *Moshe Rabbenu*, Moses our rabbi. The whole Torah is said to come from him and he becomes the guardian of the tradition. In apocryphal writings, he is exalted and made a hero. In the New Testament, Moses is mentioned more than any other figure in the Hebrew Bible (80 times). It is assumed that he is the giver of the Law. The life and activity of Jesus is often seen to be modelled on Moses, especially in Matthew's Gospel, but also in John's account of the feeding of the multitude. Yet the parallels suggest that however highly Moses is esteemed, Jesus is esteemed more highly, as for example in the story

---

Yahweh

Jews are reluctant to name the name of God. Naming, in the ancient world, could suggest control over and possession of someone – and indeed was used in magic. God is always greater than our image of him.

Where 'the Lord' is usually used in English translations of the Bible, the Hebrew has the four letters (the tetragrammaton) YHWH. In ancient Hebrew there are no vowels shown. To remind readers to say Adonai (the Lord) instead of the Holy Name, the vowels from Adonai came to be written with the consonants YHWH. Christians, unaware of scribal practice, put these vowels with the consonants, which in German became JHW(orV)H, to get the terms Jehovah and Yahweh, which are incorrect and offensive to Jews.

of the Transfiguration. In Islam, Moses is highly regarded as the first recipient of a book of revelation and he serves as the model for Muhammad, who is the 'seal' of the prophets.

The period of the judges and the kings saw the struggle against idolatry and Baal worship. The continuing importance of King David in Jewish life – and indeed in Christian tradition – needs to be noted. The link between Jewish life and the Land should be remembered and has gained renewed significance in this century. Judaism is not just a personal matter, but the religion of a community. Any community needs physical space – *Lebensraum*. Even so, the Jews survived the destruction of Jerusalem both in 593 BCE and 70 CE.

The development of rabbinic Judaism

Ezra

Ezra has been called a 'Second Moses' or 'the Father of Judaism'. That the Jews survived the destruction by the Babylonians is in part thanks to his work. There is some uncertainty whether Ezra was active before or after Nehemiah.

Nehemiah, whose first term as governor was from 445 to 433 BCE, helped re-establish the Jewish community and rebuilt the walls of Jerusalem and the Temple, although on a far more modest scale. We should picture a small Jewish city with only very limited autonomy under Persian rule.

27. Benjamin West's picture of Moses viewing the Promised Land

When Ezra arrived the situation was discouraging. Religious laxity was prevalent, the Law was widely disregarded, public and private morality was at a low ebb and intermarriage with foreigners posed the threat that the community would lose its identity and succumb to the prevailing polytheism. (Anyone who accepted the Covenant, whether Israelite-born or Gentile who renounced their previous allegiances, were classed as Jews.) Ezra was a priest and 'a scribe skilled in the law'. He represented the position of the stricter Babylonian Jews who had themselves kept the Law and who were upset by reports of laxity in Judah.

Ezra seems to have presented the Law to the people at the Feast of Tabernacles, which occurs in the autumn. He made obedience to the Law central to Jewish life. He also persuaded the people to renounce their foreign wives, since Jewish descent is through a Jewish mother. The people entered a solemn covenant to enter into no more mixed marriages, to refrain from work on the Sabbath, to levy on themselves an annual tax to support the Temple and to comply with the Law.

Although the High Priest continued to exercise authority, increasingly leadership moved to the scribes. The Torah rather than the Temple became the focal point of Jewish life. This meant that when the Temple was destroyed by the Romans, Jewish life was able to survive thanks to the leadership of the rabbis who united the people around the observance of Torah. Later rabbis claimed that it was Ezra who convened the Great Assembly and thereby created a new class of lay interpreters – *Soferim* or scribes. The scribes seem to have been a larger group, some of whom were Pharisees.

The Pharisees and rabbis

The Pharisees, contrary to much Christian preaching, made a creative contribution to the understanding of God. The origins of the movement are obscure, but the general view now is that by the first century BCE they were bringing about profound and lasting changes in Judaism.

The Pharisees had a new perception of God as concerned for the individual. God was not just the God of Abraham, Isaac and Jacob, not just the God of the nation. He watched over and cared for each member of the people of God.

Everyone, therefore, and not just the priests, should observe the Torah, which they applied to contemporary life by giving oral interpretations of it. The Pharisees gave new names to God, such as 'The Holy One' or 'Our Father who art in heaven'. They developed the synagogue as a centre of teaching, whereas the Sadducees, a small group of influential individuals, including the hereditary priests, controlled the Temple. The Pharisees, unlike the Sadducees, believed in the resurrection of the body and the world to come.

After the destruction of Jerusalem in 70 CE by the Romans, it was the descendants of the Pharisees – known as the Rabbis – led by Rabbi Johanan ben Zaccai, who as we have seen began a very creative period of interpretation of scriptures, which was to determine the character of rabbinic Judaism until the present day. It was faithfulness to Torah which preserved the Jewish people's identity through the long centuries of dispersion, despite recurrent persecution, exile and pogrom.

With the conversion of the Roman Emperor Constantine to Christianity, pressure on Jews began to increase. During the 380s, under Emperor Theodosius I, religious uniformity became the official policy. Christian mobs started to attack synagogues. By the late fourth and fifth centuries, Jews had had all their privileges withdrawn and were excluded from state office and the army. Intermarriage with Christians was punishable by death.

Babylon

In Babylonia, which was a centre of Jewish learning, Jews also suffered periodic attacks. Some Persian monarchs, however, favoured the Jews and when the Persians invaded Palestine and occupied Jerusalem in 624 CE, the local Jews received them warmly. Five years later the city was recaptured by the Byzantines and many Jews were massacred.

Under Islam

In that same year, the Prophet Mohammed completed the conquest of Mecca. Very quickly the influence of Islam spread in the Eastern Mediterranean area. The Byzantines were decisively defeated at the battle of Yarmuk in 636. Within four years, the Muslims occupied all Palestine and most of Syria. Soon Iraq and Persia were overrun by Muslim armies. By the early eighth century, the Iberian peninsula was captured by Muslims whose rule now stretched from the south-western tip of Europe to Asia Minor. In 750, the Ummayads were overthrown and replaced by the Abbasid dynasty of caliphs, who ruled from Baghdad. The *dhimmi* or subservient peoples were guaranteed religious toleration, judicial autonomy and exemption from military service as well as security of life and property, but had to acknowledge the supremacy of Islam and pay taxes.

Under Islam many Jews settled in cities and took employment in such crafts as tanning, dyeing, weaving, silk manufacture and metal-work. Jewish merchants and bankers established a network of contacts in Muslim cities. They started to travel widely, even beyond Muslim territory. Their knowledge of Arabic literature stimulated a revival of Hebrew language and literature.

During the first centuries of Islamic rule, leadership of Diaspora Jewry remained in the hands of the Babylonian exilarch, who was recognized in the caliphate as the representative of the Jews. The academy president was known as the gaon and his rulings were sought by communities throughout the Diaspora. These gaonic responses are a major source of information about Jewish life at that time. When Benjamin of Tuleda, a Jewish traveller from Spain, who wrote a *Book of Travels*, visited Baghdad in 1170, he found 40,000 Jews living there in security, with twenty-eight synagogues and ten yeshivot, or places of study.

Spain, however, by that time had the most vigorous Jewish settlement. Under the Visigoth kings, Jews in Spain had suffered severe discrimination. They, therefore, co-operated with the Muslims who invaded Spain in 711. Large and wealthy Jewish communities were soon established in Cordoba, Granada, Toledo and Seville. Elsewhere in Europe, where conditions during the so-called 'Dark Ages' were much less favourable, most Jews lived in towns or cities and played an important role in what economic activity that there was. Increasingly they became useful to the kings of Europe, both because of their international connections and their ability to lend money.

The later Middle Ages

In the later Middle Ages the situation changed. The Crusades, designed to recapture the Holy Land, became an excuse to attack 'the enemy within' and many Jews were massacred. Malicious accusations that Jews murdered Christian children at Passover so as to use their blood for baking unleaven bread, known as the 'blood-libel', spread across much of Europe. Another popular superstition was that Jews would steal the wafer of the host in order to enjoy torturing the body of Christ. The papacy never condoned these superstitions and at times denounced them, but church teaching was hostile to the Jews. Jewish usefulness to kings also declined. All Jews were expelled from Britain in 1290 and from many other European states during the next two hundred years. In 1492, the year of the 'discovery' of America by Christopher Columbus, Jews were expelled from Spain and five years later from Portugal.

Jews from Spain (Sephardi) settled in different Mediterranean countries, which were mostly under Muslim control. Maimonides, for example, spent the last years of his life in Egypt.

Poland

Many Jews from Northern Europe moved to Eastern Europe, especially to Poland where on the whole they were welcome. Just as from the ninth to the eleventh centuries, Jews had been drawn to France and the Rhineland to fill an economic vacuum, so from the thirteenth to the sixteenth centuries, Poland served as a magnet to Jews (and Christians) from Germany. In 1264, Boleslav the Pious, following a wave of Tartar depredations, issued a model charter of liberties and protection for Jews, in return for immigration to sparsely populated territories. Between 1334 and 1367 King Casimir the Great amplified the inducements and soon afterwards the Grand Duke of Lithuania copied this example. A large number of Jews from North Western Europe, therefore, settled in Eastern Europe and soon outnumbered the indigenous Jews who had come originally from the Caucasus and the Crimea.

These Jewish settlers played an important role in the economic life of the area and their language, Middle High German, became the Jewish vernacular throughout the region – a language, which with the addition of some Hebrew and Slavic expressions, became known as Yiddish.

Jews in Poland were subject to mob attacks, economic jealousy and blood-libel accusations, but they had the support of the kings and the protection of the nobility. In addition, rivalry between Catholics and Protestants in sixteenth-century Poland diverted attention from the Jews. The Jewish population of Poland expanded rapidly from about 10,000 at the beginning of the sixteenth century to more than 150,000 by 1648. Poland became a great centre of rabbinic scholarship.

In 1648, Bogdan Chmielnicki led a nationalist revolt of Ukrainian Cossacks. For two months, Chmielnicki's hordes, who were Greek Orthodox, moved from one city to another slaughtering Jews, Poles, and Catholic clergy. Warfare continued for more than twenty years. Many Jews were killed and others died of famine and epidemic. Perhaps a quarter of Polish Jewry died and others fled to Germany and Holland or to Bohemia, Austria and Hungary. The period, known as 'The Deluge' eventually came to an end in 1667, but the period of prosperity, security and scholarship was never to be restored. Of the Jews who stayed in Poland some one third, about a quarter of a million people, scattered across the countryside. Many became landlords of wayside taverns and inns.

At this bleak period in the history of the Jews of Poland, two major personalities, at opposite ends of the religious spectrum, had the strength of character to inspire followers to revive Talmudic learning, on the one hand, and simple piety on the other. Rabbi Elijah ben Solomon (1720–97), known as Vilna Gaon, a man of prodigious learning, led a great revival of Talmudic study. He insisted on the common sense meaning of the text. Rabbi Israel ben Eliezer (c. 1700–60), better known as Baal Shem Tov (often abbreviated as Besht) – the 'Master of the Good Name' – inspired a form of mystical Judaism known as Chasidism, which has already been mentioned in chapter 6.

Both Baal Shem Tov and Vilna Gaon were to have a lasting influence on Judaism. The Jewish world, however, was also about to face the opportunities and dangers of the Enlightenment.

> The Besht said: 'If a man accepts everything that happens to him in this world with love, then he will have both this physical world and also the higher world of the soul'.
>
> Alan Unterman, *The Wisdom of the Jewish Mystics*, Sheldon Press, 1976, p. 48

9

Jews in the Modern World

'The Jewish people today are in the process of millenial change, the kind of change that has not taken place since the triumph of Pharisaic Judaism eighteen hundred years ago, or the emergence of the diaspora nine hundred years before that.'

Daniel Elazar, *People and Polity*, Wayne State University Press 1989, p. 475

By the late eighteenth century, there were about 2,250,000 Jews in the world, of whom 1,750,000 lived in Christian Europe. In Holland and Britain they suffered the same disadvantages as anyone else who did not profess the official religion. The Jews of Poland, numbering well over 1,000,000, also enjoyed relative freedom, mainly because of the weakness of the central government. The prosperity, security and scholarship of the period before 'The Deluge' of 1667, however, never returned. The 420,000 Jews who lived in other parts of Europe were still subject to restrictive and humiliating legislation and mostly lived in ghettos.

The rights of man

The growing emphasis of political theorists on the rights of the individual was beginning to call in question such discrimination. In Frederick the Great's Prussia, and especially in the capital, some Jews became very wealthy. Others, of whom Moses Mendelssohn, a brilliant thinker, was the most outstanding, made significant contributions to intellectual life. Restrictions began to be relaxed and the mood of toleration spread. In 1749, Gotthold Lessing's play *Die Juden* portrayed a Jew of noble character

and in 1779, Lessing wrote *Nathan der Weise*.

The small number of Jews who settled in America in the eighteenth century enjoyed full freedom from the beginning. The Swede Peter Kalm who visited New York in 1740 observed that Jews 'enjoy all the privileges common to the other inhabitants of this town and province'. American independence confirmed this position. The Declaration of Independence of 1776 asserted that 'We hold these truths to be self-evident that all men are created equal, that they are endowed by the Creator with certain unalienable rights, that among these are life, liberty and the pursuit of happiness.' It was self-evident also that these truths applied to Jews. Because the law in America was not controlled by a particular religious community, there was also no need for Jews to operate a separate legal system. They could organize themselves like any other religious congregation.

Soon the French Revolution was also to affirm that 'all men are born, and remain, free and equal in rights'. In France, however, there were long and heated debates on whether this statement included Jews. At the time, there were some 3,500 Sephardi Jews living in Bordeaux and Bayonne in comfort and security as international merchants. Another 30,000 Ashkenazi Jews lived in north-east France and engaged in petty trade and money lending. They spoke Yiddish and lived in separate communities. Many of the defenders of emancipation agreed with the stereotyped pictures of Jews, but believed that emancipation would help to change them. As Robespierre said, 'The Jews' vices are born of the degradation you have plunged them into; they will be good when they have found some advantage in so being.' Emancipation was for Jews as individuals, not for the community. The Parisian deputy Clermont-Tonnerre expressed it in a famous sentence: 'Everything for the Jews as citizens, nothing as a nation.'

The French Revolution brought real change to the Jews of France. As the armies of the French Republic spread across Europe, they brought emancipation to Jewish communities. In Italy, the French armies abolished the ghettos, whilst in the Rhineland they were warmly welcomed by the Jews who lived there. Even so, in France, Jews found themselves the objects of suspicion and criticism from Left and Right. Napoleon tried to resolve the situation by convening in 1806 an Assembly of Jewish Notables from all over the French Empire. The 111-strong body, elected by Jewish community leaders, met from July 1806 to April 1807 and provided answers to twelve questions put to it by the authorities. These concerned marriage-laws, Jewish attitudes to the state, internal organization and usury. On the basis of these answers Napoleon replaced the old communal organization with what were termed consistories, as part of a general Jewish statute which regulated the conduct of those who were now seen not as Jews but as 'French citizens of the Mosaic faith'. Napoleon supplemented the secular body by convening a parallel meeting of rabbis and learned laymen to advise on technical points of the Torah. This body became known as the Sanhedrin. It did not do much useful work. Its existence, however, led to the totally untrue suggestion that there was a secret Jewish plot to take over the running of the world – a falsity which gained some credence in the forged document known as *The Protocols of Zion*.

The nineteenth century

France

Napoleon's so-called Infamous Decree of 1808 subjected Jews in some areas of the country to discrimination, but this decree was not renewed by Louis XVIII's government in 1818. Thus by early in the nineteenth century Jews in France were free to play a full part in the life of the nation.

Britain

Jews were readmitted to Britain under Oliver Cromwell. The community was quite small and grew slowly. In the eighteenth century these Sephardi Jews, whose ancestors had been expelled from Spain, were joined by Ashkenazi Jews fleeing westwards from Poland. The need for consultation between these two communities led to the establishment of the Board of Deputies of British Jews. By the end of the eighteenth century the office of Chief Rabbi had also emerged.

By the end of the Napoleonic Wars in 1815, the Jewish community numbered between 20,000 and 30,000 people. Some two-thirds of these lived in London. No provincial community numbered more than one thousand and some were less than one hundred. There was an increasing supply of literature in English and sermons in English, if not the rule, were not uncommon.

Economically, many of the pedlars and old-clothes men had established themselves in small businesses. A few of the wealthiest Jews, such as members of the Goldsmid and Rothschild families, had entered into English society. Some Jews appeared on the stage, others became doctors or entered other professions.

During the eighteenth and nineteenth centuries, the Jewish community in Britain was gradually set free from lingering discrimination. In 1788, the courts recognized the competence of a rabbinical tribunal to regulate kosher food and, in 1793, to decide the validity of Jewish marriages.

Attempts to remove other discrimination were

for some years defeated in the House of Lords. In 1847, Baron Lionel de Rothschild was elected as one of the members of parliament for the City of London. There was no statute forbidding a Jew to sit in parliament, but the Oaths of Allegiance and Supremacy ended with the words 'on the true faith of a Christian'. The government's efforts to remove discrimination against the Jews won the support of the House of Commons but were repeatedly defeated in the Lords because of opposition led by the bishops. It was not until 26 July 1858 that Baron de Rothschild took his seat in the House of Commons – almost exactly two hundred years after Cromwell allowed Jews to return to Britain.

28. Lionel de Rothschild, the first Jewish member of Parliament

Increasingly public life and the professions were opened to those Jews who wished to enter them. Yet perhaps more than half of the Jews of Britain in the second half of the nineteenth century belonged to the working class.

From 1858 to 1881 the Jewish population almost doubled to a little over 60,000. The increase was largely due to immigration from Russia, Poland, Germany and Holland. The period from 1881 to 1914 saw an even more rapid increase in the number of immigrants – perhaps about 150,000 in all, together with many more travelling via Britain to the New World. The migrants had to subsist on their journey on the potatoes and herrings that they brought with them. Many arrived almost penniless.

Germany

The situation was different in each state. Following the Congress of Vienna, some German states revoked the privileges which had recently been granted to Jews. In 1819, many Jews were attacked during what became known as the 'Hep Hep' riots. A number of Jews converted to Christianity, including Moses Mendelssohn's youngest son and two of his daughters. Gradually during the century, Jews gained emancipation throughout Germany, although this created new problems of how to be Jewish in a changed world.

Whilst Jews in Western Europe were being freed from discriminatory legislation, Jews of Eastern Europe continued to suffer oppression and exploitation. The position of Jews in each East European country was different.

Poland

As a result of the Congress of Vienna, most of Poland's 1,200,000 Jews came under Russian rule. The official policy was to restrict Jews to the western provinces, the 'Pale of Settlement', where by the 1880s, there were some 4,000,000 Jews, most of whom spoke Yiddish and who engaged in petty trade. As heavy industry began to develop in the latter part of the nineteenth century, many Jews moved to the towns to look for work. By the end of the century, nearly one third of Warsaw's population was Jewish. In the early years of this century, there was some emancipation for Jews, but it depended where in Poland they lived. There was periodic mob violence and in between the wars, with the rise of Fascism, Jews suffered increasing pressure and growing discrimination.

Hungary

In Hungary, especially after 1867 when Hungary virtually obtained 'home rule' within the Austro-Hungarian Empire, Jews became politically and culturally assimilated. With increasing industrialization, Jews moved to the towns. By 1920, nearly half Hungary's Jews were living in Budapest. The Hungarian Jews since 1868 were divided between Orthodox Jews and 'Neolog' Jews, who had made slight changes to traditional practices.

The twentieth century: the spread of antisemitism

The comparative prosperity and freedom of Jews in much of Europe during the nineteenth century was threatened towards the end of the century by renewed massacres of Jews in Russia, known as pogroms, and by re-emerging antisemitism in Western Europe.

With the accession as Tsar of Alexander III (1881–1894), any hopes that Russian Jews had of gradual emancipation were shattered by a new pogrom. They realized that antisemitism was there to stay as official government policy and that the dream of integration was an illusion. Many Russian Jews prepared to endure yet more of the age-old suffering inflicted on their people. Others decided to leave. Large numbers made their way to the USA, although some settled in Western Europe instead. A few headed for Palestine, determined no longer to be settlers in an alien land. Despite great physical hardship, they started to create Jewish communities on the Land.

In Western Europe, the last decade of the nineteenth century saw Friedrich Nietzsche give intellectual respectability to antisemitism. In France, the limits of liberalism in that country were exposed by the Dreyfus affair, which spurred Theodor Herzl to call for a Jewish state.

In 1894 Dreyfus, a Jewish officer, was found guilty of treason on evidence which was eventually shown to be perjured. (Zola wrote a well-known letter in Dreyfus' defence called J'accuse, which got Zola himself into trouble.) Theodor Herzl, at that time a journalist, attended the ceremony of Dreyfus' degradation, which had antisemitic overtones and made the presumption that a Jew's loyalty to the state was always suspect. Although the point is disputed, Theodor Herzl, some four years later, said, 'What made me a Zionist was the Dreyfus trial.' During the summer of 1893 he wrote Der Judenstaat, which was published in 1894. He declared that there was no room or hope for Jews in Europe and that they had to acquire land on which to build a nation.

The period between the two World Wars saw the growing threat to Jews from both Fascism and Communism. It also saw the struggle to establish a Jewish homeland in Palestine despite the opposition of the Arabs who lived there and the prevarications of British policy.

After the Holocaust

Jewish life in Europe was shattered by the onslaught of the Nazis. Some six million Jews were murdered, of whom over a million were children. Synagogues were destroyed, scrolls burned, Jewish communities and culture devastated. Leadership of the Jewish world has, since the Second World War, passed to Israel and the USA.

The Jewish population of Europe had grown rapidly from 1700 to 1939. In 1700 it was about 719,000. By 1800, the figure was approximately 2,000,000. By 1900, it was 8,800,000 and by 1939 it was 9,500,000. This is an increase of over thirteen

29. Dreyfus at the court martial in Rennes

times, whereas the total population of Europe had increased by only just over four and a half times from 125,000,000 in 1700 to 575,000,000 in 1939.

In 1860, European Jews accounted for approaching 90% of the world's total. By 1945, only about 20% of the world's Jews lived in Europe. The Jewish population of Europe has continued to fall, partly because of emigration, partly because of a low birth rate and now also because of the growing number of Jewish men who marry non-Jewish women.

Poland

The widespread hostility to Jews which already existed in Poland before the German invasion may have made it easier for the Nazis to launch their murderous attack on the large Jewish population. Compared to a pre-war population of 3,500,000 Jews, there are now only about 12–15,000 Jews, many of whom are not registered as Jews. Of those Polish Jews who survived the Holocaust, many emigrated. The largest Jewish community is now in Breslau. Recent governments are trying to preserve what remains of the Jewish community and Jewish history in Poland. Diplomatic relations with Israel were established in 1990 and the Israel Philharmonic orchestra has visited Poland.

Romania

In Romania, nearly 400,000 Jews survived the Holocaust, but the present Jewish population is now only about 22,000. This is because a large number of Jews were able to leave the country, most of whom settled in Israel, which now has about 400,000 Jews of Romanian origin. Those Jews who remain have been able to live an observant Jewish life and many hundreds eat each day at the kosher restaurants which the community maintains.

In Romania, as elsewhere in Eastern Europe, the Jewish population is elderly and there are years of cultural and educational deprivation to make up. Whilst some Jews continue to leave for Israel – and

for the USA if they can gain entry – the Jewish world recognizes the need to strengthen Jewish life amongst the Diaspora of Eastern Europe. Otherwise, as Chief Rabbi Moses Rosen of Romania has warned, those Jews who stay in Eastern Europe will disappear from the ranks of the Jewish people by assimilation and become indistinguishable from the rest of the population.

Hungary

After the First World War, Hungary lost much of its territory. Jews now began to become increasingly unpopular and to suffer from antisemitism, especially as the Fascist party, the Arrow Cross, grew in strength. The first Jewish law of May 1938 ended Jewish emancipation. Even so because Hungary maintained a measure of independence until the spring of 1944, when Germany occupied Hungary, Jews for a time were spared the worst excesses of the Nazis. In one month, however, between 5 May and 7 June, 300,000 Hungarian Jews were deported to death camps in the East. Thanks to the Swedish ambassador to Hungary, Raoul Wallenberg, several thousands of the Jews of Budapest were saved from the Nazis.

The present Jewish population of Hungary of about 80,000 makes it the biggest Jewish population in Eastern Europe, apart from Russia. The majority of Hungary's Jews live in Budapest. The city has thirty synagogues and houses of prayer, of which the magnificent 130-year old main synagogue is now being restored. There is a Jewish day school, a ritual slaughter house and, most important, the only rabbinical college in Eastern Europe.

Russia

Before the revolution of 1917, the Jewish population of the Russian Empire saw itself as an ethno-religious entity and the authorities likewise had seen Jews as primarily members of a religious community. The virulent anti-religious stand of the Communist regime quickly deprived Jews of the

30. Raoul Wallenberg saved many Hungarian Jews

religious basis of their identity and sought to develop the ethnic identity instead. Yiddish schools and cultural activities gained state support. Resources were also poured into Jewish agricultural resettlement projects in Birobidzhan in Eastern Siberia, where a Jewish National Region was created in 1934. In the late thirties government policy changed and all visible manifestations of Jewish culture were effectively destroyed. Jews continued to be registered as such on official documents and were subject to discrimination against them in applying for jobs or places at the university, but at the same time deprived of the means of maintaining Jewish identity.

During the war, over 2,000,000 Jews in the Soviet Union became victims of Nazi genocide and others suffered under the Stalinist purges of the 1940s and 1950s. By the 1960s, Jews had largely been deprived of the means of maintaining both their religious and their ethnic identity and many of the second Soviet-raised Jewish generation were absorbed into the Russian-speaking population.

In the 1970s there was a steadily growing demand by some Jews to emigrate. Those who were refused permission – 'refuseniks' – gained world-wide support. Quite a number, however, did leave either for Israel or the USA. The collapse of Communist rule opened the way for mass emigration and in 1991, 185,000 Jews emigrated to Israel alone. In 1992, some 60,000 Jews left for Israel and about the same number for the West, mainly to Germany and the USA. The remaining Jewish population in Russia may be about 1,000,000 – the last Soviet census in 1989 recorded a Jewish population of 1,487,000. Nearly 90% of these are Ashkenazi, although there are some other sub-ethnic groups. Many have little knowledge of Jewish practice and if a Jewish community is to be maintained in Russia, there is a big educational task to be performed.

France

Among all Europe's Jews, it was the French Jews who were most assimilated. Chief Rabbi Zadoc Khan (b. 1839) said of the effects of the French Revolution that it seemed as though the era predicted by the prophets of Israel had finally begun. The antisemitic campaigns of the 1880s were stormy, but in the end Dreyfus was proved innocent. The French educational system, which is highly centralized, encouraged a sense of national unity.

This idyllic situation has changed for several reasons. The Vichy government's adoption of the anti-Jewish edict of 3 October 1940 excluded Jews from a whole series of social positions and denied the principle of equality before the law. The French state which for one hundred and fifty years had stood by the Jews had now betrayed them. Jews of France too did not escape the attacks of the Nazis. The existence of the state of Israel caused French Jews to rethink their position, although few French Jews emigrated to Israel.

Another significant change in Jewish life in France has been the large-scale migration of Sephardi Jews from North Africa. It is estimated that this migration has quadrupled the number of Jews in France to around 600,000, making this the largest Jewish community in Western Europe. This immigration has led to a veritable renaissance of Jewish life in southern France. Jewish identity is now clearly expressed, with increasing numbers of Jewish children attending Jewish schools.

Britain

It may be that a similar trend is taking place in Britain, where some people are beginning to speak of Jews as an ethnic minority rather than as a religious community. Spectrum Radio, for example, caters for ethnic communities and gives plenty of time to Jewish affairs. Yet to be seen as an ethnic minority is to place Jews amongst the disadvantaged and the alien. The Board of Deputies of British Jews has opposed the inclusion of a Jewish category in the question on ethnic origins in the census which is carried out every ten years. This is part of the debate about how Jews understand themselves.

When Jews returned to Britain under Oliver Cromwell, and especially in the nineteenth and early twentieth centuries, the emphasis was on becoming at home in British society. The stress in Jewish schools at the turn of the century was to help those immigrants who had recently come from Eastern Europe to become good British citizens. Now, the emphasis of Jewish education is to develop an awareness of Jewish faith, culture and identity. The key word for the present Chief Rabbi, Dr Jonathan Sacks, is continuity. He speaks of three great eras of modern Jewry. The first was integration, the second, following the Holocaust,

was survival. The challenge today, he has said, is to show that a Jew can live as a Jew.

New centres of Jewish life

USA

That there are many ways of being Jewish is especially true in the United States of America. The small number of Jews who settled during the colonial period did not suffer discrimination and in independent America they had the equal rights of any citizen. Large numbers of Jews, mainly from Eastern Europe, settled during the nineteenth cen-

31. Jewish emigrants arriving in the USA

tury. As these immigrants moved westwards, they founded new Jewish centres which were almost entirely controlled by laymen. The exigencies of life in a new and open society encouraged an openness to reform and change. During the nineteenth century, led by the Reform Jew Isaac Mayer Wise, Reform Judaism established itself.

Many of the immigrants who came at the end of that century were from very Orthodox and Chasidic communities and brought these traditions with them. Some of the main Chasidic centres are now in Brooklyn. American Jewish life has therefore been called a continuum from the most traditional Orthodoxy to the most radical Reconstructionism. We shall look in more detail at these different forms of Judaism in the next chapter.

American Jews have a powerful place in their society, both because of considerable wealth and because they have been an effective political lobby. This has ensured massive support from the USA for Israel. Individual American Jews have given generously to Israeli institutions.

Israel

The two decisive events in Jewish history in this century have been the Holocaust and the creation of the state of Israel. Both have occasioned numerous books. Here there is only space to recall the key dates in modern Israel's history.

On 9 December 1917, British forces captured Jerusalem. For the next thirty years, Palestine was to be under a British mandate. In 1917, the population of Palestine consisted of about 512,000 Muslims, 61,000 Christians and 66,000 Jews. Five weeks before the capture of Jerusalem, in the Balfour Declaration, the British government had said that it viewed with favour the wish to establish in Palestine a national home for the Jewish people, but that this was to be done without prejudicing the civil and religious rights of existing non-Jewish communities in Palestine. The contradiction inherent in the two statements meant that the inter-war years

were marked by unrest in Palestine and frequent changes of British policy. Nonetheless during this period a considerable number of Jews came to settle in the Land. By 1937, the Jewish population was about 400,000.

The situation deteriorated after the Second World War. In November 1947, the United Nations agreed to the partition of Palestine into Jewish and Arab states. This was accepted by the Jews but not by the Arabs. The British mandate expired six months later and on 14 May 1948, Ben Gurion proclaimed the state of Israel, which received immediate *de facto* recognition from President Truman of the United States. Almost immediately Israel was attacked by its Arab neighbours and there followed a desperate struggle for survival, with cruel acts on both sides. Many Arabs fled from the areas under Israeli control. By the time an armistice was signed in 1949, Israel had gained about one third more territory than the UN partition plan had allowed for. The city of Jerusalem was divided.

During its early years, Israel absorbed a large number of Oriental Jews who had come from countries under Muslim control.

The period up till 1967 was one of uneasy peace, with terrorist attacks from outside and occasionally within the country and was marked by the Suez War. The Six Day War in 1967 was a milestone. First because for a short moment the Jewish state seemed in mortal peril. Jews across the world who had not up till then been enthusiastic Zionists now identified with Israel, whilst the inaction of Christians and of Western states confirmed Jewish suspicions that as in the 1940s the rest of the world would watch in horror the destruction of Jews but take no effective action to save them. In fact, the Israelis proved victorious and gained a lot of land. This included Sinai, which was eventually returned to Egypt in exchange for recognition, and the West Bank.

There have been subsequent wars – the 1973 Yom Kippur War and the War in Lebanon. At last, with the Palestinian Liberation Organization willing to recognize the state of Israel, a peace process has begun which in 1994 gave Palestinians autonomy in Gaza and Jericho and which has led to peace with Jordan. The peace process is fraught with dangers, but it offers the hope of stability and economic growth in the area.

The question of survival, against external enemies and internal terrorist activity, has dominated Israeli life for most of its history. The period has, however, been marked by the amazing building of a new nation and the integration of Jews from many parts of the world. Hebrew is the national language and has been a force for integration as has compulsory military service. Even so, there is enormous variety in Israel of Jews from different backgrounds and of different beliefs and practices. Although only a minority of Israelis are religiously observant, the Orthodox religious community has considerable influence on national life. Non-Orthodox Judaism is largely excluded from official life. The variety in Israel emphasizes the difficulty of defining what it means to be Jewish.

The future

Reconstructing Jewish life after the Holocaust and building the state of Israel have been the dominant concerns of Jewish life for the past fifty years. As the remaining survivors of the camps die will the vividness of the horror of the Holocaust fade? As Israel is allowed to live at peace with its neighbours will the urgency of support for Israel become less of a rallying point for the Jewish world? In America and Western Europe a growing number of Jews marry out. How are Jews to understand and define their identity in the coming century? Will history and culture be enough or will there be renewed emphasis on Judaism's religious inheritance?

It would be rash to try to predict the future, but it is important to appreciate why there is vigorous debate on these matters within the Jewish community, as different Jews seek to argue for the most appropriate way of expressing their Jewish identity in a changing world.

32. David Ben-Gurion proclaims the State of Israel

10

Varieties of Judaism

'Almost all Jewish groups in Israel and the diaspora express a commitment to Jewish survival, peoplehood and unity.'
Jonathan Sacks, *One People? Tradition, Modernity and Jewish Unity,*
Littman Library 1993, p. 13

Until the nineteenth century, Judaism was essentially a unity. There had been different sects in the first century CE, such as the Sadducees or Pharisees or Essenes. In the eighth century, the Karaites, who originated in Babylon, rejected the Talmud and came to be regarded as heretical. There were different emphases and arguments between Chasidic and rabbinic leaders. Yet despite their different attitudes, all accepted scriptural law, or Torah, as binding. That is to say they accepted the same authority, even if they disagreed about the interpretation of that authority. This is no longer the case. Different groupings of Jews disagree about authority and therefore about faith and practice.

In describing the main groupings of Jews today, we shall concentrate on developments in the USA and Great Britain. In Israel, many Jews are secular and either do not observe any or only very few religious practices.

Orthodox or Traditional Judaism

So far we have used the broad categories of Orthodox and Progressive Judaism, but there are differentiations to be made within each category. The majority of practising or observant Jews tend to be called 'Orthodox', although the term was first used by Reform Jews of Traditionalist Jews. Many Orthodox Jews might rather think of themselves as

'Traditional'. They maintain the practices taught them by their parents. They accept the authority of both the written and oral Torah.

Orthodox is a term that covers many sub-groups. Some Orthodox Jews, variously labelled ultra-Orthodox, right-wing or strictly Orthodox (*haredi*) live in semi-enclosed communities, for example in Mea She'arim in Jerusalem, in Brooklyn in New York or Stamford Hill in London. Many belong to the mystical Chasidic tradition, especially to the Lubavitch branch of this.

The beginnings of organized right-wing Orthodoxy in Britain date to the end of the last century. The Federation of Synagogues was established in 1887, as a grouping of small Orthodox synagogues in the East End of London. The aim of the Federation was to ensure representation of these synagogues on communal bodies, to secure joint provision for burial at inexpensive rates and to provide spiritual leadership.

It was not until the period between the wars that the Chasidic movement became established, particularly in north and east London, with the arrival in Britain of some distinguished Chasidic rabbis.

In recent years in Britain, central Orthodoxy, comprising the United Synagogue and now the Federation of Synagogues, and the Spanish or Sephardim synagogues, although still by far the largest group, has declined. It was estimated that in 1983, the right-wing Orthodox had

33. Strictly Orthodox Jews in Mea She'arim, Jerusalem

4.4% of male membership, central Orthodox 70.5%, Sephardim 2.7% and Reform and Liberals (Progressive) 22.4%. In London, the percentage of central Orthodox would be rather lower and that of both right-wing and Progressive Jews rather higher.

Orthodox Judaism, in its various expressions, has continued to evolve and is not the same today as the Judaism from which those Jews who came to be known as Reform broke away in the last century.

Progressive Judaism

Reform Judaism

At the beginning of the nineteenth century, a German Jewish financier and communal leader called Israel Jacobson started to initiate some reforms. At the school which he established, in Seesen, Westphalia, general subjects were taught by Christian teachers. Choral singing, hymns and addresses were introduced as well as some prayers in German. In 1810, Jacobson built the first Reform Temple next to his school. Soon, he moved to Berlin and founded a temple there.

In 1817, a Reform Temple was opened in Hamburg on the initiative of Eduard Kley, who had been a preacher of the Berlin Reform group, with innovations such as prayers and sermons in German as well as choral singing and organ music. The Hamburg reformers cited the Talmud to support these changes. In 1819, they issued a prayer book which omitted repetitions and some mediaeval poems. Whilst some rabbis, such as the Hungarian Aaron Chorin, declared the changes permissible, the Orthodox reaction was hostile. In 1836, Samson Raphael Hirsch, who had been appointed Chief Rabbi of the Duchy of Oldenburg at the age of twenty-two, published *The Nineteen Letters on Judaism*, which were a defence of Orthodoxy.

Despite this opposition, the Reform movement began to grow in Germany and to spread to other countries. A first Reform synod was held in Brunswick in 1844.

In Britain, in 1836, some Spanish and Portuguese communities presented a petition asking for modifications in the service similar to those introduced at the Reform synagogue in Hamburg. The request was turned down. As a result in 1840, eighteen prominent and wealthy members of the community, in association with six members of other synagogues, decided to establish a synagogue which would be neither Ashkenazi nor Sephardi, but British. The synagogue, known as The West London Synagogue, was opened in 1842. It was to become the centre of the Reform Movement, although the growth of Reform Judaism in Britain was initially slow. It took a generation for similar synagogues to be established in Manchester and Bradford.

34. The West London Synagogue

In the USA, the first signs of Reform appeared in 1824, when a small group of congregants in Charleston, South Carolina, attempted to introduce some of the reforms which had been made in Hamburg. Following the revolutions of 1848, quite a number of Jews came to America, including some Reform Jews from Germany, who established Reform synagogues in New York. Prominent among these early reformers were David Einhorn of Har Sinai synagogue in Baltimore and Samuel Alder and Gustave Gottheil of Temple Emanuel in New York.

It was Isaac Mayer Wise, however, who was to put Reform Judaism on a firm footing in America. Born in Bohemia, he came to the USA in 1846 to accept a rabbinic post in Albany, New York. His efforts at reform provoked a violent reaction. Wise moved to Cincinnati, Ohio, where he published a new Reform prayer book, *Minhag Amerika*, as well as several Jewish newspapers. After a time, he managed to call together the first Conference of Reform Rabbis in Philadelphia in 1869. Four years later, this was followed by the founding of the Union of American Hebrew Congregations. In 1875, the Hebrew Union College, the first Reform rabbinical college to be built on American soil, was established. The principles on which American Reform Judaism were based were set out in the Pittsburgh Platform of 1885.

Reform Judaism has continued to grow and evolve. In 1972, the first woman rabbi was ordained.

Conservative Judaism

In 1845, Rabbi Zacharias Frankel, who was born in Prague, walked out of the Reform rabbinical conference in Frankfurt, intent on formulating a conservative approach to the tradition. The majority, with whom he disagreed, had voted that there was no need to use Hebrew in Jewish worship.

Subsequently, a number of American rabbis advanced a similar position and by the end of the century they had established a Jewish Theological Seminary in New York, headed by Solomon Schechter, to foster positive historical Judaism. Schechter rejected both Reform ('Lord, forgive them, for they know nothing') and Orthodoxy ('A return to Mosaism would be illegal, pernicious and indeed impossible').

Reconstructionist Judaism

Reconstructionist Judaism developed out of the thinking of an individual scholar. Mordecai Kaplan, who was born in Lithuania in 1881, came to New York in 1889. He became an Orthodox rabbi, but grew increasingly dissatisfied with traditional teaching and took a post at the Jewish Theological Seminary. In 1915 he helped to organize the New York Jewish Centre which emphasized Judaism as a civilization, a phrase which was to become the title of his book, which was published in 1935.

Humanistic Judaism

Humanistic Judaism is a recent development. It originated in 1965, when the Birmingham Temple in Detroit began to publicize its philosophy of Judaism. This affirmed that Judaism should be governed by empirical reason and human needs.

Humanistic Jewish congregations have been established in a number of major American cities and the National Federation has some 30,000 members. There are small groups in a number of other countries, such as Belgium, France, Israel, Australia and Argentina.

Two other recent approaches are worth mentioning. One called Polydoxy is propounded by Alvin Reines, Professor of Philosophy at the Hebrew Union College. Rejecting the idea of revelation, he argues that each Jew must exercise personal autonomy and decide for himself or herself what to believe and practice. The emphasis on personal freedom is also characteristic of another new approach, which is called Open Judaism.

Liberal Judaism

In Britain, a more radical alternative to Orthodoxy than Reform Judaism was Liberal Judaism, which emerged early in this century. In 1902, the Jewish Religious Union was founded. Initially this brought together Jews of various outlooks. The influence of Claude Montefiore, who advocated a universalizing of Jewish ethics was, however, too radical for Orthodox Jews, who gradually withdrew. Instead of accepting an invitation to use the facilities at the West London Reform Synagogue, it was decided eventually to create a separate Liberal Jewish Synagogue at St John's Wood. Under the influence of Montefiore and of Lily Montagu, a social worker, a new movement was born which was to become known as the Union of Liberal and Progressive Synagogues.

Unity and difference within Judaism

A description of the varieties of Judaism may over-emphasize the differences and needs to be balanced by a recognition that nearly all religious Jews share many beliefs. This is partly because disagreement amongst Jews is more often about behaviour than belief. Chief Rabbi Jonathan Sacks has said (in *The Times* of 30 June 1994) that in this there is a basic difference between Jewish and Christian faith. 'Christian faith is more a matter of what propositions you believe in, Jewish faith is more a matter of what people and traditions you belong to.'

Even so, inherent in the traditional practices, there is an often implicit framework of belief. Maimonides' *Thirteen Principles of the Faith* is widely quoted as a summary. This affirms the Unity of God, who is the Creator of all that is, to whom alone it is right to pray. God knows the deeds and thoughts of every human being and rewards those who keep the commandments. There will be a resurrection of the dead at the time chosen by God. The Principles include belief that the prophecy of Moses was true, that the Torah will never be changed and that 'though he tarry', the Messiah will come.

The Messiah

The Hebrew word *Mashiach*, for which the Greek is Christos, means anointed. The term was applied in biblical times to various individuals such as kings, priests and prophets. In Jewish thought the Messiah is not a divine being nor the object of worship.

Jewish Messianic expectation is quite varied. Some picture a historical figure, perhaps King David, who brings in a new age of peace and justice. Some emphasize the person of the Messiah, whilst others focus on the coming Messianic Age. Some see this in political terms, whilst others emphasize its spiritual nature. Some emphasize the Messiah's role in giving Israel pre-eminence over the nations, whilst others stress his universal task. At different periods, there has been speculation that a historical figure, such as Rabbi Akiva or Bar Kokhba in the second century CE, or Shabbatai Zevi in the seventeenth century, was the promised Messiah.

Despite the variety, the belief expresses confidence that God's kingdom will come, that one day God's rule will become operative in the life of humankind. This hope is evident in the liturgy and has sustained Jews in times of trial. It has also inspired the great variety of Jewish activity for the welfare of others. The hope is based on faith in God, but men and women are called to prepare for the coming of the Messianic Age.

> I believe, I believe, I believe
> with a perfect faith
> in the coming of the Messiah;
> in the coming of the Messiah I believe.
> And even though he tarry
> I nevertheless believe.
> 　　　　Even though he tarry,
> Yet, I believe in him,
> I believe, I believe, I believe.
>
> 　　Verse written by an unknown Jew on a wall
> 　　　　in the besieged Warsaw ghetto

The concept of being a 'chosen' people is also understood in different ways, but it affirms the belief that Jews have a special place in God's purposes and have been called to be a holy people. The terrible sufferings of the Holocaust have led many Jews in recent years to reflect deeply on their vocation.

Zionism

Part of God's promise to his people was the land of Israel. Through long years of exile Jews continued to remember Zion in their prayers, and through the centuries a small Jewish community lived in the Holy Land, Eretz Israel.

Not all Jews initially supported the Zionist movement, but today most Jews have a strong sense of identity with Israel, even if they may be critical of particular actions of Israeli governments. Jews see Israel as a place where they can fulfil the command to be a holy people, a refuge from Gentile oppression, and a sign of God's continuing mercy.

There has been in Israel a great flowering of Jewish culture. Political problems, however, have created tensions between the efforts to create a just democratic society and to defend the state from hostile neighbours and terrorist activity.

Internal differences

Although Jews of different traditions share a framework of belief, as well as a common history, calendar and rituals, there are significant differences.

Orthodox Jews believe that both the written and oral Torah are directly revealed by God. Non-Orthodox Jews hold that the oral Torah is capable of revision to adapt it to modern life, for example, in the way the Sabbath is observed. They accept historical criticism of the Bible.

Progressive Jews do not expect nor pray for the restoration of the Temple and sacrificial system. They hope for a coming 'Messianic Age' rather than the advent of a personal Messiah. They do not believe literally in the resurrection of the dead, although they retain the hope of life after death and speak of the immortality of the soul.

In Progressive synagogues, men and women sit together and women may be rabbis. The use of musical instruments is welcomed in Progressive synagogues.

Orthodox Jews tend to regard theirs as the only correct and authentic form of Judaism, whereas Progressive Jews accept that there are various expressions of Judaism.

These are broad categorizations. Some Jews who are members of Orthodox synagogues may share Progressive views on some subjects, whilst some Progressive Jews may have traditional attitudes on some subjects. If you talk to some Jews you will probably find they do not fit neatly into categories. In many religious communities, the actual beliefs of members may differ from official statements of belief. The variety is a sign of the vitality with which Jews are responding to the modern world.

The Holocaust and the creation of the state of Israel have presented major challenges to Judaism. Jews too, like members of all religions, face the various challenges of the modern world, of which the climate seems unsympathetic to all traditional religions. Is the answer to stand firm on the tradition or to try to adapt it to modern thought? There is, clearly, a wide spectrum of answers to this question.

11

A New Relationship

'Many men and women have worked and are still working today, on both sides, to overcome old prejudices and to secure ever wider and fuller recognition of that "bond" and that "common spiritual patrimony" that exists between Jews and Christians.'

Pope John-Paul II

Until the middle of this century, the great majority of Jews lived in Europe, where Christianity has been the dominant religion. In the USA, which now has the largest number of Jews, the majority religion is Christianity. Both in the past and even today the life of many Jews has been and is deeply affected by the attitudes of their Christian neighbours.

The relationship of Jews and Christians is long and complex. The Hebrew Bible is part of the Christian scriptures. The two religions have influenced each other through the centuries. At times, there have been friendly relations between some Jews and Christians; but too often the relationship has been painful. In this century, especially since the Second World War and the horror of the Holocaust, there has been a patient effort by some Jews and Christians to build a new creative relationship. This has involved working together to root out prejudice and antisemitism, purging Christian teaching of anti-Jewish elements, which in turn has led to a new Christian self-understanding, and replacing mission by dialogue.

Antisemitism

It is helpful to try to distinguish between antisemitism, anti-Zionism and anti-Judaism.

The word antisemitism only dates back to the nineteenth century, although the phenomenon is at least as old as Roman times. In 1879, the German propagandist Wilhelm Marr coined the term antisemitism to describe pseudo-scientific theories that the Jews were a pernicious racial element that needed to be eliminated from Western civilization.

In Roman times, Jews were often disliked, partly because they did not conform to the behaviour patterns of others. They were particularly unpopular in Alexandria – the Passover story was not flattering about the Egyptians! Jews were said to be lepers, to worship the head of an ass, to commit cannibalism and to hate all humanity. There was, however, no theory that Jews were racially inferior. That is a recent development which was carried to extreme lengths by the Nazis.

Anti-Zionism

Zionism is the movement to establish a Jewish state. Some people have criticized Zionism, either because they think a country should not be based on a particular religion or because of sympathy for the Palestinians. It is possible to be anti-Zionist without being antisemitic, but anti-Zionism is often used as a cover by antisemites. It is also possible to criticize particular actions of the Israeli government without being anti-Zionist.

35. An antisemitic poster used by French Nazis

Anti-Judaism

Although some writers use the term 'Christian antisemitism', others use 'Anti-Judaism' to distinguish Christian preaching against Jews from other forms of prejudice. Anti-Judaism has caused enormous suffering. It is based on a theological position, now rejected by the churches, not on a racist ideology. The dominant view in the church, until the last half century, has been that the new covenant replaced the old covenant. It was claimed that with the resurrection of Jesus, the church, the 'new Israel' or 'new people of God', became the heir to the promises made to Abraham and the patriarchs long ago. By its rejection of Jesus ('its long awaited Messiah'), Israel had shown itself unfaithful and had reneged on the covenant. In punishment, God destroyed the holy city of Jerusalem and banished the Jews from the Promised Land. Jews were accused of the crime of deicide – killing God – and abused as 'Christ killers'. Often they were regarded as children of the devil and various libellous stories circulated about them.

> 'For many centuries, primitive Christian Europe had regarded the Jew as the "Christ killer", an enemy and a threat, to be converted and so to be "saved", or to be killed, to be expelled, or to be put to death with sword and fire.'
>
> Martin Gilbert, *The Holocaust*, Collins 1986, p. 19

On 9 November 1938, a pogrom was launched throughout Germany during which nearly 600 synagogues were set alight and many Jews were attacked. Jewish shop windows were smashed and as a result the night became known as 'the night of broken glass', Kristallnacht. Fifty years later memorial meetings were held in many cities, in which many Christians took part.

> 'The travesty of Kristallnacht and all that followed is that so much was perpetrated in Christ's name. To glorify the Third Reich, the Christian faith was betrayed . . . And even today there are many Christians who fail to see it as self-evident. And why this blindness? Because for centuries Christians have held Jews collectively responsible for the death of Jesus. On Good Friday Jews have, in times past, cowered behind locked doors for fear of a Christian mob seeking "revenge" for deicide. Without the poisoning of Christian minds through the centuries, the Holocaust is unthinkable.'
>
> Robert Runcie, then Archbishop of Canterbury, at the London Kristallnacht Commemoration, 1988

36. A man dying of starvation at Belsen

37. A Holocaust memorial at Dallas, USA

A new relationship

Aware of the pernicious influence of Christian anti-Jewish teaching, a number of Jews and Christians, since the Second World War, have laboured to correct centuries of misunderstanding.

A new understanding of the relationship of Christianity to Judaism has been expressed in changes to the liturgy and by official statements by several churches. For the Roman Catholic Church, the decisive turning point was the decree *Nostra Aetate* of the Second Vatican Council, promulgated in October 1965. Many Protestant Churches have also agreed statements on Christian-Jewish relations. In 1988, the Lambeth Conference of bishops of the Anglican communion also produced a document about relations with Jews and Muslims.

> The Jews still remain most dear to God because of their fathers, for He does not repent of the gifts He makes nor of the calls He issues. In company with the prophets and the Apostle Paul, the Church awaits that day, known to God alone, on which all peoples will address the Lord in a single voice and 'serve Him with one accord'.
>
> Since the spiritual patrimony common to Christians and Jews is thus so great, this sacred Synod wishes to foster and recommend that mutual understanding and respect which is the fruit above all of biblical and theological studies, and of brotherly dialogues.
>
> *Nostra Aetate* 1965, §4

There is now wide agreement that:

1. The Covenant of God with the Jewish people remains valid.

2. Antisemitism and all forms of the teaching of contempt for Judaism, especially teaching about deicide, are to be repudiated.

3. The living tradition of Judaism is a gift of God.

4. Coercive proselytism directed towards Jews is incompatible with the Christian faith.

5. Jews and Christians bear a common responsibility as witnesses to God's righteousness and peace in the world.

Jesus the Jew

Jesus' own solidarity with the Jewish people is stressed. He came to fulfil, not to abrogate the Jewish life of faith based on the Torah and the prophets.

At the beginning of this century many Christians had largely forgotten that Jesus was a Jew. Pictures of Jesus in popular devotional art gave no hint of this. Gradually, thanks in part to the work of Jewish scholars, the Jewishness of Jesus has been recognized and historical studies have tried to see his ministry in a Jewish milieu. Questions about the historical Jesus are complicated and much debated.

A growing number of scholars now see Jesus as a faithful Jew rather than someone in opposition to the Judaism of his day. This is partly because the traditional Christian picture of the Pharisees is now thought to be untrue. It seems likely that the bitterness recorded in the Gospels reflects the sharp polemic between the Early Church and the Pharisees which was taking place at the time the Gospels were written, rather than the words of Jesus himself.

The Pharisees do not appear to have been involved in the death of Jesus. It may be that some of the Sadducees or High Priestly party wanted Jesus out of the way and colluded with the Romans. It is important to remember that Jesus was put to death by the Romans. Crucifixion was a Roman penalty. It is known that Pilate was a cruel ruler. Anyone who was said to claim to be a king was likely to be in trouble with the Roman authorities. Jesus had considerable support. He was arrested at night, probably to avoid a public outcry. When he was crucified, some Jews mourned and lamented over him (Luke 23.27, 48). His first disciples were all Jewish. The historical accuracy of the accounts of Jesus' trial by the Sanhedrin are questioned by many scholars.

It is suggested that the break between church and synagogue was gradual. Jewish life rested at the time on four pillars:

1. The role of the Temple at the centre of Israel's national and religious life.

2. The centrality of Torah.

3. The belief that Israel had been specially chosen by God.

4. The belief that God is one.

Gradually amongst those who believed in Jesus these beliefs were eroded. As the membership of the church became predominantly Gentile, attention came to focus on Jesus Christ rather than on his own message that 'The Kingdom of God is at hand'. The title 'Son of God' was also given a rather different emphasis by Gentile believers.

Covenant

Many Christians used to believe that the New Covenant replaced the Old Covenant. This view is sometimes labelled 'supercessionism' or 'replacement theology'. It is now rejected on various grounds. Partly because such a view calls in question God's trustworthiness and faithfulness to his promises. It also ignores the continuing faithfulness of many Jews to the Torah and the spiritual vitality of Judaism. It probably misrepresents Jesus' attitude to Torah and may misrepresent Paul's. Increasingly churches recognize that the Jews continue to be 'people of God'.

This has led many Christians to question traditional claims that there is no salvation outside the church and to ask whether Jews need to believe in Jesus to be saved.

This in turn has led to a change of attitude towards mission to the Jews. Christians disagree on whether they should try to convert Jews, and the situation is further complicated by Messianic Jews, especially 'Jews for Jesus', who claim to be Jews who accept Jesus as Messiah. Many Christians now reject aggressive evangelism and repudiate proselytism. Instead they emphasize the importance of dialogue. This includes efforts really to appreciate and understand the faith and practice of the other as well as discussion both of questions of belief and ethics. Increasingly there is the hope that Christians and Jews can together witness to the ethical values that they share.

We have a common message. Our world needs to hear of a God who is at once a God of love and a God of justice. A God who cares for the creation and for every human being made in God's image. A God who has committed to human beings the care of the world and made them trustees of the earth and all that is in it. A God who has put within us the vision of a kingly reign and bidden us share in its coming.

Sermon preached by Lord Coggan,
former Archbishop of Canterbury,
at a service to mark the 50th anniversary of the
founding of The Council of Christians and Jews

Conclusion

With the immediate memory of the Holocaust fading and the reconstruction of Judaism partly achieved, with the hope that Israel will be able to live at peace with its neighbours and with traditional hostility from Christians being replaced by understanding, Jews may find that the greatest dangers to Judaism today may be internal Jewish divisions rather than external hostility and the temptation to assimilate to the surrounding secular society. Jews may also find that the world is now receptive to the values and beliefs that they have treasured for many centuries, so that they can fulfil the biblical calling to be a light to the Gentiles and share in the repairing of the world.

38. The Pope is welcomed to the Rome synagogue

Bibliography

Alexander, Philip S., *Textual Sources for the Study of Judaism*, Manchester University Press 1984

Black, Naomi (ed), *Celebration: The Book of Jewish Festivals*, Collins 1987

Braybrooke, Marcus, *Children of One God: A History of CCJ*, Vallentine Mitchell 1991

Braybrooke, Marcus, *Time to Meet*, SCM Press and Trinity Press International, PA 1990

Cantor, Norman, *The Sacred Chain: A History of the Jews*, HarperCollins 1995

Charlesworth, James H., *Jesus within Judaism*, SPCK 1988

Cohen, Jeffrey, *Horizons of Jewish Prayer*, United Synagogue 1986

Cohn-Sherbok, Dan, *The Jewish Heritage*, Basil Blackwell 1988

Cohn-Sherbok, Dan, *The Crucified Jew: Twenty Centuries of Christian Antisemitism*, Harper Collins 1992

Cohn-Sherbok, Dan, *A Dictionary of Judaism and Christianity*, SPCK 1991

Cohn-Sherbok, Dan, *Holocaust Theology*, Lamp Press 1989

de Lange, Nicholas, *Judaism*, Oxford University Press 1986

Dunn, James D. G., *The Partings of the Ways*, SCM Press and Trinity Press International, PA 1991

Epstein, Isidore, *Judaism: A Historical Presentation*, Penguin 1959

Forta, Arye, *Judaism*, Heinemann Educational 1989

Friedlander, Albert, *A Thread of Gold*, SCM Press and Trinity Press International, PA 1990

Goldberg, David and Rayner, John, *The Jewish People: Their History and Religion*, Penguin 1989

Hilton, Michael and Marshall, Gordian, *The Gospels and Rabbinic Judaism*, SCM Press 1988

Jones, Pamela Fletcher, *The Jews of Britain*, The Windrush Press 1990

Kung, Hans, *Judaism*, SCM Press and Crossroad Publishing Co., New York 1992

Maccoby, Hyam, *Judaism in the First Century*, Sheldon Press 1989

Magonet, Jonathan, *A Rabbi's Bible*, SCM Press 1991

Neusner, Jacob, *Telling Tales: Judeo-Christian Dialogue*, Westminster John Know, Louisville 1993

Pawlikowski, John, *What are they saying about Christian–Jewish Relations?*, Paulist Press, New York 1980

Romain, Jonathan A., *Faith and Practice: A Guide to Reform Judaism Today*, Reform Synagogues of Great Britain 1991

Romain, Jonathan A., *The Jews of England*, Michael Goulston Foundation 1988

Sanders, E. P., *Paul and Palestinian Judaism*, SCM Press and Fortress Press, Minneapolis 1977

Sanders, E. P., *Jesus and Judaism*, SCM Press and Fortress Press, Minneapolis 1985

Sanders, E. P., *Judaism: Practice and Belief 63 BCE– 66 CE*, SCM Press and Trinity Press International, PA 1992

Shanks, Hershel (ed), *Christianity and Rabbinic Judaism*, SPCK 1993

Solomon, Norman, *Judaism and World Religion*, Macmillan 1991

Swidler, Leonard (ed), *Bursting the Bonds: A Jewish–Christian Dialogue on Jesus and Paul*, Orbis Books, Maryknoll 1990

Ucko, Hans, *Common Roots: New Horizons*, World Council of Churches, Geneva 1994

Unterman, Alan, *Jews: Their Religious Beliefs and Practices*, Routledge & Kegan Paul 1981

Uris, Leon, *Exodus* (fictional account of the birth of the state of Israel), William Kimber 1959

Vermes, Geza, *Jesus the Jew*, SCM Press and Fortress Press, Minneapolis, 3rd edn 1994

Vermes, Geza, *The Religion of Jesus the Jew*, SCM Press and Fortress Press, Minneapolis 1993

Webber, Jonathan, *Jewish Identities in the New Europe*, Littman Library of Jewish Civilization 1994

Wilson, Marvin R., *Our Father Abraham*, William B. Eerdmans, Grand Rapids 1989

Wouk, Herman, *The Hope*, Hodder and Stoughton 1993

Zuidema, Willem, *God's Partner: An Encounter with Judaism*, SCM Press 1987

Glossary

The literal meaning of each word is given in brackets. Hebrew words in the explanation are translated if they do not appear elsewhere in the glossary.

Adar
Hebrew month occurring around March; Purim is on the 14th Adar.

Aleinu (it is our duty)
Prayer concerning the duties of Israel, occurring towards the end of all daily, Sabbath and festival services.

Aliyah; plural: *Aliyot* (going up)
The honour of being called to recite the blessing over the Torah during a service; it can also mean emigration to Israel.

Amidah (standing)
Central prayer in all daily, Sabbath and festival services; also known as the Shmoneh Esreh (the eighteen benedictions) and the Tefillah (the prayer).

Arba kanfot (four corners)
Garment with tzitzit on each of its four corners, worn in fulfilment of the command in Numbers 15.39; also known as tallit katan.

Ashkenazi (biblical place name)
Term now used for Jews originating from Central and Eastern Europe.

Bar/batmitzvah (son/daughter of the commandment)
Ceremony for boys and girls aged thirteen in which they are called to read from the Torah in acknowledgment of the beginnings of Jewish adulthood.

Barchu (bless)
Prayer in all daily, Sabbath and festival services calling the worshippers to bless God.

Bat chayil (daughter of worth)
Group ceremony in Orthodox synagogues for girls aged twelve, involving prayers and readings in acknowledgment of their Jewish adulthood.

Bedeken (covering)
Ceremony immediately prior to a wedding in which the groom places the veil on the bride to ensure there is no mistake as to her identity, as happened in the case of Jacob in Genesis 29.25.

Beth Din (court of law)
Rabbinic court, nowadays primarily concerned with supervising status cases, such as conversion, adoption and divorce.

Bikkur cholim (visiting the sick)
The meritorious act of visiting anyone who is ill.

Bimah (raised position)
Platform upon which is the reading desk in synagogue.

Birkat ha'mazon (blessing over meals)
Thanksgiving for food.

Brit milah (covenant of circumcision)
Ceremony in which a boy's foreskin is removed when he is eight days old in fulfilment of Genesis 17.10.

Challah: plural: *challot* (bread)
Plaited loaf used at the Sabbath, as a symbol of the sustenance God gave the Israelites whilst in the wilderness.

Chametz (leaven)
Food that contains leaven and therefore which may not be eaten during the festival of Passover, based on Exodus 12.15.

Chanukah (dedication)
Festival that usually occurs in December celebrating the re-dedication of the Temple by the Maccabees in 167 BCE and the survival of the Jewish faith despite attempts to destroy it by the Assyrians.

Chanukat ha'bayit (dedication of one's home)
Ceremony of affixing a mezuzah to one's new home.

Chanukiah
Nine-branched candelabra used at Chanukah.

Chasidim; adjective: *Chasidic* (pious ones)
Jewish sect founded in Eastern Europe in the late eighteenth century as a revivalist movement, now part of the ultra-Orthodox establishment.

Chavurah; plural: *chavurot* (group)
Small association of like-minded individuals who meet together for prayer, study and Jewish celebrations.

Chazan; plural: *chazanim* (cantor)
Trained singer who leads congregational prayers.

Chevra Kaddisha (holy brotherhood)
Burial society that carries out the washing and shrouding of a Jewish corpse.

Chumash (five)
The printed edition of the Five Books of Moses.

Chuppah (canopy)
Cloth draped over four poles, under which a bride and groom stand during their wedding ceremony.

Churban (destruction)
A reference to the Holocaust, in which six million Jews were murdered; also known as the Shoah.

Cohen (priest)
A descendant of the high priest Aaron, and still having a priestly role in Orthodox synagogues today.

Diaspora (dispersion)
Any land in which Jews live outside Israel.

Dreidl (spinning top)
Children's toy used at the festival of Chanukah, with four Hebrew letters on its side standing for 'A Great Miracle Happened There'.

Elul
Hebrew month prior to *Rosh Hashanah*, characterized by spiritual preparations for the oncoming New Year.

Eretz Yisrael
The land of Israel.

Eshet chayil (a woman of worth)
Poem recited by men on Friday evening in praise of their wives, taken from Proverbs 31.

Get; plural: *gittin* (bill of divorce)
Document certifying the religious divorce of a couple.

Haftarah (conclusion)
Reading from the Prophets that supplements the *Torah* portion at Sabbath and festival services.

Haggadah (narration)
Book read at the Passover meal which recounts the Exodus from Egypt.

Halakhah; adjective: *halakhic* (the path)
Jewish Law as derived from the Bible and rabbinic literature.

Havdalah (separation)
Ceremony that concludes the Sabbath, and marks the beginning of the working week; also performed at the close of festivals.

Kaddish (sanctification)
Prayer at the end of daily, Sabbath and festival services in praise of God; has come to be regarded as a memorial prayer, with names of the deceased often mentioned beforehand.

Kashrut (appropriate food)
The dietary laws concerning forbidden and permitted foods.

Kavvanah (concentration)
The act of concentrating on the meaning of prayers that one is reciting rather than saying them by rote.

Kedushah (holiness)
The third paragraph of the Amidah.

Kehillot (congregation)
A Jewish community.

Keriah (cutting)
The act of tearing a piece of clothing worn by a mourner shortly before a funeral.

Ketubah (document)
The marriage contract signed by a bride and groom, and read out at the wedding ceremony.

Kiddush (sanctification)
Blessings over bread and wine made before Sabbath and festival meals.

Kippah (covering)
Head covering that is either worn continuously or just during prayer.

Kittel (gown)
White robe worn at the High Holy Days, by a groom at

his marriage, and by the leader of a seder.

K'lal Yisrael (the unity of Israel)
The notion that all Jews are bound to each other as part of the same people, whatever their religious, cultural, or geographical differences.

Kol Nidrei (all vows)
Name given to the service on the eve of Yom Kippur, taken from the opening words of the prayer that starts the service.

Kosher (fit)
Food that is permissible for Jews to eat according to the dietary laws.

Knesset (gathering)
The parliament of the state of Israel.

Kvatter (godfather)
Person who hands a baby boy to a mohel for circumcision.

Kvatterin (godmother)
Person who brings a baby boy from his mother into the room where he will be circumcised.

Lag ba'Omer (33rd day of the counting of the Omer)
Minor festival traditionally associated with happy events during an otherwise mournful period; often chosen as a date for weddings.

Lulav (palm)
Used generally to refer to the palm, willow and myrtle branches that are bound together and waved at Sukkot.

Maccabee
Family who led the Jewish revolt against the Assyrians, leading to the rededication of the Temple in 167 BCE.

Machzor (cycle)
The festival prayer book.

Maftir (concluding)
The last of the seven portions into which the weekly Torah reading is divided according to the annual cycle.

Magen David (shield of David)
Jewish symbol, now part of the flag of Israel.

Mazeltov (good luck)
Term of congratulations.

Menorah (candelabra)
Seven-branched candlestick that was used in the Temple.

Mezuzah (doorpost)
Container with the first two paragraphs of the Shema inside attached to the front door of one's home and other rooms.

Mikveh (gathering of water)
Ritual bath used privately by those converting to Judaism, by women following their menstrual period, or by a bride and groom before their wedding.

Minyan (quorum)
The presence of ten adult males which, traditionally, is required in order for certain prayers to be said publicly.

Mi-sheberach (may He who blesses)
Blessing given after performing a mitzvah in a synagogue service.

Mishnah; adjective: *mishnaic* (learning)
Rabbinic commentary on the Bible completed around 200 CE.

Mitzvah; plural: *mitzvot* (command)
One of the 613 commandments; also a good deed; also an honour in a synagogue service.

Mizrach (east)
Plaque on the eastern wall of a house, indicating the direction of Jerusalem.

Mohel; plural: *mohalim* (circumciser)
Person who performs a circumcision.

Ner Tamid (eternal light)
Light above the ark in synagogue that is always on, reminiscent of the menorah in the Temple; now often also regarded as a reminder of the eternal presence of God.

Nisan
Hebrew month occurring around April; Passover is on 15th Nisan.

Omer, Counting of the (a measure)
The forty-nine day period between Pesach and Shavuot; originally offerings from the barley harvest were brought each day to a Temple and counted.

Parashah (portion)
A section from the weekly reading of the Torah.

Pesach (Passover)
Festival celebrating the Exodus from Egypt.

Pidyon ha'ben (redemption of the first born)
Ceremony in which traditionally a first born boy is presented to a priest and then redeemed by his father.

Pikuach nefesh (saving of life)
The ruling that all prohibitions (excluding idolatry, incest and murder) may be ignored in order to preserve human life.

Purim (lots)
Festival celebrating the deliverance of the Jews of Persia from Haman's attempts to kill them.

Rosh Hashanah (Head of the Year)
The Jewish New Year.

Sandek (companion of the father)
Person who holds a baby boy whilst it is being circumcised.

Sanhedrin (council)
Assembly of 71 elders that met in Jerusalem and was the supreme legislative body in ancient Israel.

Seder; plural: *Sedarim* (order)
The service surrounding the Passover meal.

Selichot (supplications)
Penitential prayers recited shortly before the New Year.

Semichah (laying of hands)
Ordination ceremony for Rabbis.

Sephardi (biblical place name)
Term now used for Jews originating from the Spanish peninsula and the Mediterranean.

Shabbat (Sabbath)
The day of rest, beginning at sunset on Friday evening.

Shabbateanism
Seventeenth century movement that considered Shabbetai Zvi to be the Messiah; it was discredited after his conversion to Islam, although some adherents maintained their belief.

Shalom Aleichem (peace be with you)
Song on Friday evening to welcome the Sabbath.

Shavuot (weeks)
Festival celebrating the revelation at Mount Sinai.

Shechitah (slaughter)
Jewish method of killing animals for food as quickly and painlessly as possible.

Sheloshim (thirty)
The first month of mourning after the loss of a close relative.

Shema (hear)
Quotation from Deuteronomy 6.4–9, 11.13–21 and Numbers 15.37–41 recited in all morning and evening services.

Shemini Atzeret (eighth day of assembly)
The additional eighth day of Sukkot in the Orthodox calendar, but combined with Simchat Torah by the Reform.

Sheva brachot (seven blessings)
Blessings recited at a marriage ceremony.

Shivah (seven)
The first week of mourning after the loss of a close relative.

Shofar (horn)
The horn of a kosher animal, often a ram, used at the New Year and Day of Atonement.

Shul
Yiddish term for synagogue.

Siddur (order)
Prayer book.

Simchat Torah (rejoicing of the law)
Festival immediately after Sukkot marking the end of the cycle of readings from the Pentateuch, by reciting the last chapter of Deuteronomy and immediately starting a new cycle of readings with the first chapter of Genesis.

Sofer; plural: *soferim* (scribe)
Person responsible for writing the Hebrew text of ritual objects such as a Torah, mezuzah and tefillin.

Sukkot (Tabernacles)
Festival commemorating the wanderings of the Israelites in the wilderness, and the time of the fruit harvest.

Taharah (purification)
Ritual washing of a dead body.

Tallit (gown)
Prayer shawl.

Tallit katan (small gown)
Undergarment with tzitzit on each of the four corners; also known as arba kanfot.

Talmud (learning)
Rabbinic commentary on the Mishnah; repository of Jewish Law completed around 500 CE.

Tefillin (prayer boxes)
Leather boxes containing the Shema worn on one's head and arm in conformity with Deuteronomy 6.8.

Terefah (torn)
Generally used to refer to food that is not fit for consumption by Jews.

Tevilah (immersion)
Immersion in a mikveh or river, generally by a proselyte for conversion, or by a woman at the end of her menstrual period.

Tikkun olam (repairing the world)

Restoring the world to the state of harmony that existed in the Garden of Eden.

Tish'ah B'-Av (ninth of Av)
   Fast day commemorating the destruction of the First and Second Temples in Jerusalem, and other tragedies in Jewish history.

Torah (teaching)
   The five books of Moses; also used to refer to the entirety of Jewish teaching.

Tu B'Shevat (fifteenth of Shevat)
   The New Year for Trees; the time at which saplings are planted and existing trees are tithed.

Tzedakah (righteousness)
   Charity.

Tzitzit (fringes)
   The fringes on the four corners of a tallit.

Yahrzeit (time of year)
   The anniversary of a person's death.

Yeshivah (academy)
   Institution for Jewish studies, primarily concentrating on the Talmud.

Yigdal (may He be magnified)
   Song at the end of Sabbath and festival evening services, summarizing Maimonides' Thirteen Principles of Faith.

Yihud (togetherness)
   The time a bride and groom spend alone together immediately after their marriage; originally the time of consummation.

Yizkor (may He remember)
   Memorial service for those who have died, held on Yom Kippur and at other times.

Yom Ha'atzma'ut (day of independence)
   Israel Independence Day.

Yom Kippur (day of atonement)
   Day spent in prayer, repentance and fasting.

Yom Ha'Shoah (day of destruction)
   Fast day commemorating the victims of the Holocaust.

Zemirot (songs)
   Melodies particularly associated with Sabbath table songs.

Index

Aaron ben Asher, 49
Abbasid dynasty, 59
Abduraham, 14
Abraham, 11, 29, 30, 52, 53, 56, 58
Achad Ha-am, 26
Adam, 11, 56
Ahasuerus, 20
Akhenaten, 54
Akiva, Rabbi, 11, 12, 49, 76
Alder, Samuel, 75
Alexander the Great, 18
Alexander III, 64
Amenophis IV, 54
Antiochus IV Epiphanes, 18, 28
Aten IV 54

Balfour, Arthur, 70
Ball Shem Tov, 41, 60
Bar Kochba, 12, 76
Ben-Gurion, David, 22, 70
Benjamin of Tuleda, 59
Besht, 41, 60
Birnbaum, Philip, 50
Blue, Rabbi Lionel, 50
Boleslav the Pious, 60
Buber, Martin, 51

Casimir the Great, 60
Charlap, A Hyman, 50

Chmielnicki, Bogdan, 60
Chorim, Aaron, 74
Clermont-Tonnerre, 62
Coggan, Donald, 82
Columbus, Christopher, 59
Constantine, Emperor, 58
Cordovero, Rabbi Moses, 41
Cyrus, 52

David, King, 57, 76
Dreyfus, 64, 68

Einhorn, David, 75
Elazar, Daniel, 61
Elijah, 10, 29
Elijah ben Solomon, 60
Esther, 19, 20, 21
Ezekiel, 50
Ezra, 20, 46, 52, 57, 58

Frankel, Zacharias, 75
Frederick the Great, 61

Gamaliel III, Rabbi, 41
Gedaliah, 21
Gilbert, Martin, 79
Goldsmid, 62
Gottheil, Gustave, 75
Guigui, Rab Abraham, 26

Hagar, 53
Halevi, Judah, 13, 51
Haman, 20, 21
Herod the Great, 18
Herzl, Theodor, 22, 64
Heschel, Abraham, J., 27
Hillel, 48
Hillel II, 13
Hirsch, Samuel Raphael, 74

Isaac, 52, 53, 56, 58
Ishmael, 53
Israel ben Eliezer, 60

Jacob, 52, 53, 54, 56, 58
Jacobson, Israel, 74
Jesus, 27, 81, 82
Jethro, 54
Johanan ben Zakkai, Rabbi, 48, 58
Jonah, 16, 17
Joseph, 54
Judah ha-Nasi, 49
Judah Maccabee, 18

Kalm, Peter, 61
Kaplan, Mordecai, 10, 75
Küng, Hans, 6

Leah, 54
Leibniz, 50
Lessing, Gotthold, 61
Lot, 53
Louis XVIII, 62
Luria, Rabbi Isaac, 41, 51

Magonet, Rabbi Jonathan, 50
Maimonides, Moses, 49, 50, 59, 76
Marr, Wilhelm, 78
Mattathias, 18
Meir, Rabbi, 48
Mendelssohn, Moses, 51, 61, 63
Montagu, Lily, 76
Montefiore, Claude, 76
Mordecai, 20

Mosco, Maisie, 2
Moses, 9, 13, 37, 43, 44, 46, 49, 52, 54, 56, 76
Muhammad, 57, 59

Napoleon, 62
Nebuchadnezzar, 21
Nehemiah, 20, 21, 37, 57
Nietzche, Friedrich, 64
Noah, 11

Oneklos, 49

Pharaoh, 52, 54
Pontius Pilate, 82

Rachel, 54
Ramesses II, 54
Rashi, 49, 50
Rayner, Rabbi John, 28
Reines, Alvin, 75
Robespierre, 62
Romain, Rabbi Jonathan, 26, 45
Rosen, Chief Rabbi Moses, 66
Rosenweig, Franz, 51
Rothschild, 62
Rothschild, Lionel de, 63
Runcie, Robert, 79

Sacks, Jonathan, 69, 72, 76
Sarah (Sarai), 53
Schechter, Solomon, 75
Sethos I, 54
Shabbatai Zevi, 76
Shammai, 48
Simchah ben Samuel Vitry, 50
Simeon ben Yochai, Rabbi, 12
Simeon, Rabbi, 49
Singer, Revd Simeon, 50
Solomon, Rabbi Norman, 44
Spinoza, Baruch, 50

Terah, 53
Theodosius I, Emperor, 58
Thuthmosis III, 54
Truman, President, 70

Ummayads, 59

Vashti, 20
Vilna Gaon, 60

Wallenberg, Raoul, 68
Wiesel, Elie, 51
Wise, Isaac Meyer, 70, 75

Xerxes I, 20

Zipporah, 54
Zola, 64
Zuidema, Willem, 26